GIFTED
GAMES™

COGAT® TEST PREP
GIFTED AND TALENTED TEST PREPARATION
Level 9

Gateway Gifted Resources™
www.GatewayGifted.com

Thank you for selecting this book. We are a family-owned publishing company - a consortium of educators, test designers, book designers, parents, and kid-testers.

We would be thrilled if you left us a quick review on the website where you purchased this book!

The Gateway Gifted Resources™ Team
www.GatewayGifted.com

TABLE OF CONTENTS

ABOUT THIS BOOK: This book helps prepare children for the COGAT® Level 9, a test given to third graders. Not only will this publication help prepare children for the COGAT®, these logic-based exercises may also be used for other gifted test preparation and as critical thinking exercises. This book has five parts.

1. Introduction (p.4-9): About this book & the COGAT®, Test Taking Tips, Points Tracking, and Question Examples

2. Practice Test 1 (Workbook Format) (p.10-54): These pages are designed similarly to content tested in the COGAT®'s nine test question types. Unless your child already has experience with COGAT® prep materials, you should complete Practice Test 1 (Workbook Format) together with no time limit. **Before doing this section with your child, read the Question Examples & Explanations (p.6-9).**

3. Practice Test 2 (p.55-91): Practice Test 2 helps children develop critical thinking and test-taking skills. It provides an introduction to standardized testing in a relaxed manner (parents provide guidance if needed) and an opportunity for children to focus on a group of questions for a longer time period (something to which some children are not accustomed). This part is also a way for parents to identify points of strength/ weakness in COGAT® question types. Practice Test 2 is divided into three sections to mirror the three COGAT® batteries: Verbal, Quantitative, and Non-Verbal.

4. Answer Keys (p.92-95): These pages contain the Practice Test answers as well as brief answer explanations.

5. Afterword (p.96): Information on additional books, free practice questions, and your child's certificate

ABOUT THE COGAT® LEVEL 9: The COGAT® (Cognitive Abilities Test®) test is divided into 3 "batteries."
- *Verbal Battery; total time: around 30 minutes*
Question Types (10 minutes each, approximately): Verbal Analogies, Verbal Classification, Sentence Completion
- *Non-Verbal Battery; total time: around 30 minutes*
Question Types (10 minutes each, approximately): Figure Analogies, Figure Classification, Paper Folding
- *Quantitative Battery; total time: around 30 minutes*
Question Types (10 minutes each, approximately): Number Series, Number Puzzles, Number Analogies

The test has 170 questions total. The test, about two hours in length, is administered in different testing sessions. Children are not expected to finish 170 questions in one session. **See pages 6 to 9 for details on question types.**

ABOUT COGAT® TESTING PROCEDURES: These vary by school. Tests may be given individually or in a group. These tests may be used as the single factor for admission to gifted programs, or they may be used in combination with IQ tests or as part of a student "portfolio." They are used by some schools together with tests like Iowa Assessments™. Check with your testing site to determine its specific testing procedures.

QUESTION NOTE: Because each child has different cognitive abilities, the questions in this book are at varied skill levels. The exercises may or may not require a great deal of parental guidance to complete, depending on your child's abilities, prior test prep experience, or prior testing experience. Most sections of the Workbook begin with a relatively easy question. We suggest always completing at least the first question together, ensuring your child is not confused about what the question asks or with the directions.

"BUBBLES" NOTE: Your child will most likely have to fill in "bubbles" (the circles) to indicate answer choices. Show your child how to fill in the bubble to indicate his/her answer choice using a pencil. If your child needs to change his/her answer, (s)he should erase the original mark and fill in the new choice.

SCORING NOTE: Check with your school/program for its scoring procedure and admissions requirements. Here is a general summary of the COGAT® scoring process. First, your child's raw score is established. This is the number of questions correctly answered. Points are not deducted for questions answered incorrectly. Next, this score is compared to other test-takers of his/her same age group (and, for the COGAT®, the same grade level) using various indices to then calculate your child's stanine (a score from one to nine) and percentile rank. If your child achieved the percentile rank of 98%, then (s)he scored as well as or better than 98% of test-takers. In general, gifted programs accept scores of *at least* 98% or *higher*. Please note that a percentile rank "score" cannot be obtained from our practice material. This material has not been given to a large enough sample of test-takers to develop any kind of base score necessary for percentile rank calculations.

TEST TAKING TIPS

• **Be sure your child looks carefully at each answer choice.** COGAT® questions can be quite challenging. Even if your child thinks (s)he knows the answer - (s)he should look at each choice.

• **Have your child practice listening carefully.** Paying attention is important - test questions are not repeated.

• **Test-takers receive points for the number of correct answers.** If your child says that (s)he does not know the answer, (s)he should first eliminate any answers that are clearly incorrect. Guess instead of leaving a question blank.

• **In the Workbook section, go through the exercises together by talking about them:** what the exercise is asking the child to do and what makes the answer choices correct/incorrect. This will familiarize your child with working through exercises and will help to develop a process of elimination (getting rid of incorrect answer choices).

• **Remember common sense tips like getting enough sleep.** It has been scientifically proven that kids perform below their grade level when tired. **Feed them a breakfast for sustained energy and concentration** (complex carbohydrates and protein; avoid foods/drinks high in sugar). Have them use the restroom prior to the test.

POINTS TRACKING

To increase child engagement and to add an incentive to complete book exercises, a game theme accompanies this book. As your child completes the Practice Tests, (s)he earns 1 point per question. After completing all pages, (s)he will have earned 340 points. (S)he will receive a certificate at the end (p.96). However, feel free to modify as you see fit the number of questions your child must complete in order to receive his/her certificate. Some parents may want to offer a special treat as well for completion, although this is at the parent's discretion.

WE NEED <u>YOUR</u> HELP! *(For kids and parents to read together.)*

We've got a challenge for you! Are you up for it?

This book is filled with mind-bending, challenging questions, and we need your help to answer them.

For every question you answer, you earn 1 point.

So far, the highest score anyone has ever earned is 340 points. Do you have what it takes to earn 340? Use the space below to track your points.

The questions start on page 10. Your parent (or other adult) will let you know what you need to do. Remember to:

• try to answer the questions the right way (instead of trying to finish really fast)
• pay attention
• look closely at all choices before choosing an answer
• keep trying even if some questions are hard

POINTS TRACKING

Date	Points		Date	Points		Date	Points
_____	_____		_____	_____		_____	_____
_____	_____		_____	_____		_____	_____

QUESTION EXAMPLES & EXPLANATIONS   This section introduces the nine COGAT® question types with simple examples/explanations.

VERBAL BATTERY

1. VERBAL ANALOGIES   Directions: Look at the first set of words. Try to figure out how they belong together. Next, look at the second set of words. The answer is missing. Figure out which answer choice would make the second set go together in the same way that the first set goes together.

toe > foot : petal > ?	stem	bee	leg	flower	colorful

Explanation   Here are some strategies to help your child select the correct answer:
• Try to come up with a "rule" describing how the first set goes together. Take this rule, apply it to the first word in the second set. Determine which answer choice makes the second set follow the same "rule." If more than one choice works, you need a more specific rule. Here, a "rule" for the first set is that "the first word (toe) is part of the second word (foot)." In the next set, using this rule, "flower" is the answer. A petal is part of a flower.
• Another strategy is to come up with a sentence describing how the first set of words go together. A sentence would be: A toe is part of a foot. Then, take this sentence and apply it to the word in the second set: A petal is part of a ?. Figure out which answer choice would best complete the sentence. (It would be "flower.")
• Ensure your child does not choose a word simply because it *has to do with* the first set. For example, choice A ("stem") *has to do with* a petal, but does not follow the rule.

The simple examples will introduce your child to analogical thinking. Read the "Question" then "Answer Choices" to your child. Which choice goes best? (The answer is underlined.)

Analogy Logic	Question	Answer Choices (Answer is Underlined)			
• Antonyms	On *is to* Off -as- Hot *is to* ?	Warm	Sun	<u>Cold</u>	Oven
• Synonyms	Big *is to* Large -as- Horrible *is to* ?	Tired	Stale	Sour	<u>Awful</u>
• Whole: Part	Tree *is to* Branch -as- House *is to* ?	Street	Apartment	<u>Room</u>	Home
• Degree	Good *is to* Excellent -as- Tired *is to* ?	Boring	<u>Exhausted</u>	Drowsy	Slow
• Object: Location	Sun *is to* Sky -as- Swing *is to* ?	<u>Playground</u>	Monkey Bars	Sidewalk	Grass
• Same Animal Class	Turkey *is to* Parrot -as- Ant *is to* ?	Worm	<u>Beetle</u>	Duck	Spider
• Object: Creator	Painting *is to* Artist -as- Furniture *is to* ?	<u>Carpenter</u>	Tool	Chair	Potter
• Object: Container	Ice Cube *is to* Ice Tray -as- Flower *is to* ?	Petal	<u>Vase</u>	Smell	Florist
• Tool: Worker	Paintbrush *is to* Artist -as- Microscope *is to* ?	Telescope	<u>Scientist</u>	Lab	Fireman
• Object: 3D Shape	Ball *is to* Sphere -as- Dice *is to* ?	Line	Square	Cone	<u>Cube</u>
• Object: Location Used	Jet *is to* Sky -as- Canoe *is to* ?	Boat	Paddle	<u>Water</u>	Sail
• Object: Location Used	Chalk *is to* Chalkboard -as- Paintbrush *is to* ?	Artist	<u>Easel</u>	Paint	Eraser

2. VERBAL CLASSIFICATION   Directions: Look at the three words on the top row. Figure out how the words are alike. Next, look at the words in the answer choices. Which word goes best with the three words in the top row?

cake   bread   muffin

A. bakery   B. sherbet   C. cookie   D. syrup   E. sugar

Explanation   Come up with a "rule" describing how they're alike. Then, see which answer choice follows the rule. If more than one choice does, you need a more specific rule.
• At first, test-takers may say the rule for the top words is that "they are all a kind of food." However, more than one answer choice would fit this rule. A more specific rule is needed. A more specific rule would be that "the foods are baked foods." Therefore, the best answer is "cookie."
• Ensure your child does not choose a word simply because it has to do with the top three. For example, choice A (bakery) has to do with the three, as all three could be found at a bakery. However, "bakery" is not a baked food. Another simple example:

fall   spring   summer

A. warm   B. season   C. month   D. winter   E. weather

This example demonstrates a common mistake. Note answer choice "B", season. Here, the question logic (or, rule) is "seasons." A child, having the rule "seasons" in their mind, may mistakenly choose "season." However, the answer is "winter," because "winter," like the top three words, is an *example* of a season.

Below are additional simple examples to introduce your child to classification logic.

- function and uses of common objects (i.e., writing and drawing / measuring / cutting / drinking / eating)
Fork / Chopsticks / Knife   Choices: Stove / Straw / Meat / <u>Spoon</u>   (Used For Eating)
- location of common objects
Refrigerator / Cabinet / Table   Choices: Bed / Restaurant / <u>Oven</u> / Shower   (Found In Kitchens)
- appearance of common objects (i.e., color; objects in pairs; objects with stripes vs. spots; object's shape)
Ketchup / Blood / Firetruck   Choices: <u>Cherry</u> / Mustard / Cucumber / Police car   (Red)
- characteristics of common objects (i.e., hot, cold)
Ice / Igloo / Popsicle   Choices: Cookie / <u>Snowman</u> / Palm Tree / Coffee   (Cold)
- animal types
Leopard / Cheetah / Kitten   Choices: Elephant / Giraffe / <u>Tiger</u> / Bat   (Cats)
- natural habitats
Swamp / River / Pond   Choices: Desert / Mountain / House / <u>Ocean</u>   (Water)
- food growing location (i.e., on a tree, under the ground as a root, or on a vine)
Potato / Carrot / Onion   Choices: <u>Radish</u> / Melon / Pepper / Broccoli   (Root Vegetables)
- professions, community helpers
Doctor / Fireman / Vet   Choices: Witch / Wizard / <u>Teacher</u> / Baby   (Community Helpers)
- clothing (i.e., in what weather it's worn; on what body part it's worn)
Crown / Cowboy Hat / Cap   Choices: Necklace / <u>Helmet</u> / Gloves / Ring   (Worn On Head)
- transportation (i.e., where things travel, land/water/air; do they have wheels?)
Cruise Ship / Yacht / Kayak   Choices: <u>Canoe</u> / Port / Dock / Jeep   (Travel On Water)

3. SENTENCE COMPLETION Directions: First, read the sentence. There is a missing word. Which answer choice goes best in the sentence? (Read the sentences and choices to your child. They may read along silently.)

If you aren't _____ with the vase, it will break.
A. careless   B. careful   C. clear   D. risky   E. sloppy

Explanation Here, your child must use the information in the sentence and make inferences (i.e., make a best guess based on the information) and select the best answer choice to fill in the blank. Be sure your child:
- pays attention to each word in the sentence and to each answer choice
- after making his/her choice, (s)he re-reads the complete sentence to ensure the choice makes the *most* sense compared to the other choices (the answer is B)

NON-VERBAL BATTERY

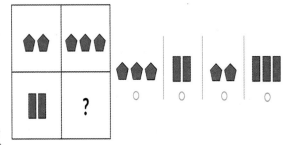

4. FIGURE ANALOGIES Directions: Look at the top set of pictures. They go together in some way. Look at the bottom set. The answer is missing. Figure out which answer choice would make the bottom set go together in the same way that the top set goes together.

Explanation Come up with a "rule" describing how the top set is related. This "rule" shows how the figures in the left box "change" into the figures in the right box. On the left are 2 pentagons. On the right are 3 pentagons. The rule/change is that one more of the same kind of shape is added. On the bottom are 2 rectangles. The first choice is incorrect, it shows 3 pentagons (not the same shape). The second choice is incorrect (it only shows 2 rectangles). The third choice is incorrect - it has 2 pentagons. The last choice is correct. It has one more of the same shapes from the left box.

Here is a list of <u>basic</u> Figure Analogy "changes." (Test questions include this logic, but questions are more challenging.)

1. Color

2. Size

3. Amount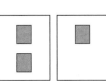

4. Color Reversal

5. Whole: Part

6. Number of Shape Sides

7. Rotation: 90° clockwise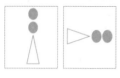

8. Rotation: 90° counter-clockwise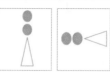

9. Line Direction

10. Flip / Mirror Image

11. Two Changes: Rotation & Quantity

12. Two Changes: Rotation & Color

5. FIGURE CLASSIFICATION

Directions: The top row of pictures is alike in some way. Which picture on the bottom row goes best with the pictures on top?

Explanation Try to come up with a "rule" describing how the figures in the top row are alike. Then, see which choice follows the rule. If more than one choice would, then a more specific rule is needed. Here is 1 white triangle, 1 lightly shaded triangle, and 1 dark triangle. These are alike because they are all triangles. The first choice is correct because it's a triangle. None of the other are.

Below is a list of basic characteristics to analyze in Figure Classification questions.

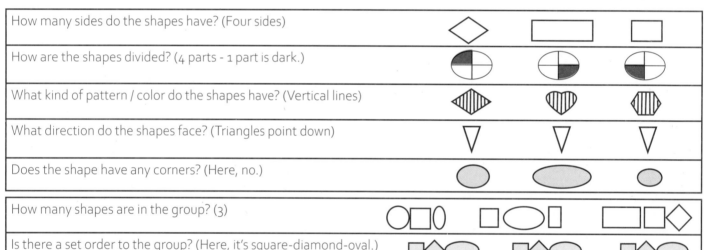

How many sides do the shapes have? (Four sides)	
How are the shapes divided? (4 parts - 1 part is dark.)	
What kind of pattern / color do the shapes have? (Vertical lines)	
What direction do the shapes face? (Triangles point down)	
Does the shape have any corners? (Here, no.)	
How many shapes are in the group? (3)	
Is there a set order to the group? (Here, it's square-diamond-oval.)	

6. PAPER FOLDING

Directions: The top row of pictures shows a sheet of paper. It was folded, then holes were made in it. Which bottom row picture shows how the unfolded paper would look?

Explanation The first choice shows how it would look - 2 holes in the correct position. In the second choice, the holes are too close to the edge. In the third and fourth choices, there's only 1 hole.
• Make sure your child pays attention to: how many times the paper is folded, the number of shapes cut out, where these shapes are on the paper, and the direction they are facing.
• If possible, do a few examples with real paper and a hole puncher.
• Below are some basic examples to introduce Paper Folding logic.

Question (How Paper Is Folded) ... Answer

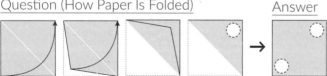

Note that 1 fold creates 2 holes.

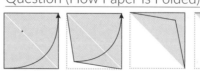

Note the change in direction of the triangle once unfolded.

8

Question (How Paper Is Folded)	Answer	Question (How Paper Is Folded)	Answer

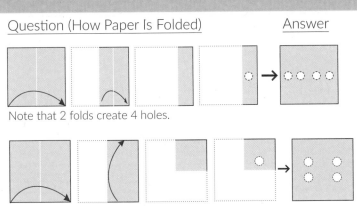

Note that 2 folds create 4 holes.

Note the change in direction of the triangles once unfolded.

Note that 2 folds create 4 holes.

Note the change in direction of the "points" once unfolded.

QUANTITATIVE BATTERY

7. NUMBER PUZZLES Directions: What answer choice should you put in the place of the question mark so that both sides of the equal sign total the same amount?

Explanation These questions have two formats. The first example is a fairly standard math problem and self-explanatory. In the second example, your child should first replace the black shape with its number value. If your child gets stumped on any Number Puzzles, (s)he can always test out each answer to find the one that works.

1. $10 = 25 - ?$ A. 25   B. 15   C. 20   D. 5   E. 0

2. $? = \blacklozenge + 2$ A. 1   B. 2   C. 3   D. 0   E. 4

    $\blacklozenge = 1$

8. NUMBER SERIES Directions: Which answer choice would complete the pattern? (Number Series have two formats: an abacus or number/text.)

1.

Abacus Explanation (#1) The last abacus rod is missing. Before it, the rods have made a pattern. Complete the pattern with the correct answer choice. We see that with each rod the number of beads increases by 1. The rods go: 1–2–3–4–5– ? This means that the missing rod needs 6 beads (Choice D).

Text Explanation (#2) The numbers have made a pattern. To help your child figure out the pattern, have them write the difference between each number and the next. In this basic example, the pattern is: -2. In easier questions, the

2.   15   13   11   9   7   ?

A.1   B.3   C.5   D.6   E.4

difference between all consecutive numbers is the same (i.e., the difference between 15 & 13 = 2 and between 13 & 11 = 2). However, sometimes the difference will not continuously repeat itself, as in these examples:

9	8	6	5	3	2	?	The pattern is: -1, -2, -1, -2, etc. & the answer is 0.
1	2	4	7	11	16	?	The pattern is: +1, +2, +3, +4, etc. & the answer is 22.
4	5	9	4	5	9	?	The pattern is: 4-5-9 & the answer is 4.

9. NUMBER ANALOGIES Directions: Look at the first two sets of numbers. Come up with a rule that both of these sets follow. Take this rule to figure out which answer choice goes in the place of the question mark. (Number Analogies have two different formats (see #1 and #2).)

1.

2	→	3
6	→	7
9	→	?

Explanation Come up with a rule to explain how the first number "changes" into the second. It could use addition, subtraction, multiplication, or division. Have your child write the rule by *each* pair. Make sure it works with *both* pairs. The rule for #1 is "+1", so 10 is the answer. The rule for #2, a bit more complicated, is "÷ by 2", so 7 is the answer.

A.8   B.3   C.1   D.10   E.4

2. [10 →5]   [8 →4]   [14 →?]   A.2   B.7   C.28   D.16   E.1

HELP ANYA FIGURE OUT HOW TO COMPLETE THE ANALOGY!

Directions *(Read these out loud to your child. (S)he may read along silently.)* Look at the first set of words. Try to figure out how they belong together. Next, look at the second set of words. The answer is missing. Figure out which answer choice would make the second set go together in the same way that the first set goes together.

Parent note: Analogies compare sets of items, and the way they are related can easily be missed. Work through these together with your child so (s)he sees how the first set is related. Together, try to come up with a "rule" to describe how the first set is related. Then, in the second set, look at the first word. Take this "rule," use it together with the first word, and figure out which of the answer choices would follow that same rule. For answer choices that do not follow this rule, eliminate them. If your child finds that more than one choice follows this rule, then try to come up with a rule that is more specific.

Example (#1): How do the words "cow" and "milk" go together? What is a rule that describes how they go together? A cow makes milk. Milk is a food made by a cow. Look at the word "bee". Which of the choices follow this rule? What food do bees make? Honey.

1   **cow → milk : bee →**

  ○ syrup   ○ sting   ○ hive   ○ flower   ○ honey

2   **teacher → students : coach →**

  ○ reporters   ○ games   ○ players   ○ principals   ○ schools

3   **frog → tadpole : butterfly →**

  ○ wing   ○ caterpillar ○ worm   ○ moth   ○ cocoon

4   **left → right : above →**

  ○ right   ○ beyond   ○ ground   ○ below   ○ basement

5   chef → meal : painter →

○ brush   ○ artist   ○ easel   ○ paper   ○ painting

6   car → gas : oven →

○ hot   ○ batteries   ○ stove   ○ cook   ○ electricity

7   food → hungry : water →

○ thirsty   ○ liquid   ○ starving   ○ drink   ○ full

8   brother → son : sister →

○ mother   ○ child   ○ daughter   ○ kid   ○ girl

9   read → magazine : listen →

○ microscope   ○ ears   ○ volume   ○ radio   ○ plot

10   hear→ here : dear →

○ dame   ○ dare   ○ deer   ○ deal   ○ dirt

11   slide → playground : camel →

○ animal   ○ ride   ○ desert   ○ horse   ○ forest

12   concert → musician : movie →

○ actor   ○ cashier   ○ theater   ○ cartoon   ○ photographer

13   terrible → bad : great →

○ quality   ○ amazing   ○ acceptable   ○ right   ○ good

14   cow → mammal : toad →

    ○ alligator   ○ frog   ○ fish   ○ amphibian   ○ reptile

15   flowers → bouquet : minutes →

    ○ alarm   ○ hour   ○ seconds   ○ math   ○ watch

16   pretty → beautiful : small →

    ○ medium   ○ tiny   ○ less   ○ size   ○ nice

17   false → true : narrow →

    ○ wide   ○ thin   ○ straight   ○ small   ○ length

18   heat → warm : rain →

    ○ water   ○ liquid   ○ drink   ○ cold   ○ damp

19   lemon → tree : tomato →

    ○ vegetable   ○ vine   ○ leaf   ○ seed   ○ salad

20   eggs → carton : flowers →

    ○ florist   ○ tree   ○ petal   ○ vase   ○ plant

21   liquid → solid : bright →

    ○ light   ○ shine   ○ beam   ○ lazer   ○ dim

22   farm → tractor : outer space →

    ○ astronaut   ○ spaceship   ○ helicopter   ○ telescope   ○ space suit

HELP ANDY FIGURE OUT WHICH WORD BELONGS WITH THE GROUP!

Directions: *(Read these out loud to your child. (S)he may read along silently.)* Look at the three words on the top row. Figure out how the words are alike. Next, look at the words in the row of answer choices. Which word goes best with the three words in the top row?

Parent note: As you did with Verbal Analogies questions, together, try to come up with a "rule" to describe how the top three words are alike and go together. Then, take this "rule," and figure out which of the answer choices would best follow that same rule. If your child finds that more than one choice follows the rule, then (s)he should try to come up with a rule that is more specific.

Example (#1): How do the words "strawberry", "apple", and "lemon" go together? What is a rule that describes how they go together? These are all fruit. Which of the answer choices would follow this rule? Blueberry.

1   **strawberry**   **apple**   **lemon**

    ◯ celery   ◯ lettuce   ◯ honey   ◯ blueberry   ◯ pepper

2   **piano**   **drums**   **trumpet**

    ◯ conductor   ◯ concert   ◯ violin   ◯ theatre   ◯ microphone

3   **cheese**   **yogurt**   **ice cream**

    ◯ dessert   ◯ fruit   ◯ ice   ◯ milk   ◯ juice

4   **backpack**   **purse**   **suitcase**

    ◯ jacket   ◯ sack   ◯ trip   ◯ cart   ◯ store

5   **telescope**   **glasses**   **magnifying glass**

○ microscope   ○ science   ○ detective   ○ eyelid   ○ window

6   **fall**   **winter**   **spring**

○ April   ○ snow   ○ February   ○ autumn   ○ month

7   **barn**   **nest**   **aquarium**

○ bird   ○ fish   ○ web   ○ basket   ○ pet

8   **airplane**   **glider**   **helicopter**

○ train   ○ truck   ○ car   ○ bus   ○ jet

9   **Asia**   **Europe**   **North America**

○ Central America   ○ Africa   ○ north   ○ China   ○ Russia

10   **lemon**   **corn**   **sunflower**

○ banana   ○ lime   ○ farmer   ○ lettuce   ○ cucumber

11   **stem**   **bud**   **leaf**

○ garden   ○ root   ○ nest   ○ log   ○ dirt

12   **elf**   **witch**   **wizard**

○ pilot   ○ doctor   ○ fairy   ○ teacher   ○ astronaut

13   **butterfly**   **grasshopper**   **ant**

○ worm   ○ snail   ○ spider   ○ turtle   ○ ladybug

14   stove   refrigerator   cabinet

○ bed   ○ sink   ○ shower   ○ bathtub   ○ sofa

15   carrot   radish   onion

○ orange   ○ pear   ○ cherry   ○ potato   ○ lettuce

16   knee   hip   ankle

○ palm   ○ elbow   ○ thigh   ○ wrist   ○ shoulder

17   windshield   wheel   engine

○ speed   ○ hood   ○ road   ○ driver   ○ fast

18   ostrich   rooster   owl

○ egg   ○ butterfly   ○ parrot   ○ feather   ○ bat

19   pond   stream   sea

○ rain   ○ tub   ○ sink   ○ spa   ○ bay

20   tennis   volleyball   hockey

○ team   ○ coach   ○ soccer   ○ tournament   ○ court

21   triangle   circle   square

○ prism   ○ pyramid   ○ cube   ○ pentagon   ○ sphere

22   Canada   Germany   Japan

○ India   ○ Pacific   ○ New York   ○ Africa   ○ Asia

HELP KELLY FIGURE OUT THE ANSWERS!

Directions
(Read these out loud to your child. (S)he may read along silently.)
First, read the sentence. There is a missing word. Next, look at the row of answer choices below the sentence. Which word would go best in the sentence?

Parent Note
At first glance, these questions may seem similar to fill-in-the-blank questions that test vocabulary acquisition. However, you will notice that the language used in some questions is actually quite simple. This section of the book helps build your child's **reasoning skills** as well.

1 **When the ____ tiger growled and clawed at its cage, we could see its sharp teeth.**

   ○ friendly   ○ silly   ○ warm   ○ fierce   ○ soft

2 **My dad wants to ____ a workshop in our backyard where he plans to store tools and work on projects.**

   ○ draw   ○ destroy   ○ calculate   ○ construct   ○ remove

3   Alex hid his candy under his bed so that nobody would ____ it.

  ○ ignore   ○ discover   ○ miss   ○ cover   ○ hide

4   This rain shower was quite unexpected because it ____ rains in the desert.

  ○ seldom   ○ often   ○ quietly   ○ clearly   ○ frequently

5   Following the ____ hike, Sophie was exhausted, and her muscles had become quite sore.

  ○ easy   ○ relaxed   ○ demanding   ○ simple   ○ sunny

6   Max was ____ because he did not prefer one contestant or the other.

  ○ neutral   ○ even   ○ above   ○ excited   ○ basic

7   The ____ chemicals the factory dumped into the river have been terrible for wildlife.

  ○ safe   ○ toxic   ○ healthy   ○ harmless   ○ clean

8   The ____ space between the buildings prevented our truck from passing through.

○ passable   ○ large   ○ limited   ○ perfect   ○ strong

9   Freddie had slept so little in the past week that he ____ to rest.

○ refused   ○ yearned   ○ disliked   ○ suspected   ○ declined

10   It is difficult to ____ what homes would have looked like thousands of years ago.

○ handle   ○ access   ○ feel   ○ visualize   ○ reach

11   Anya found animals so ____ that she visited the zoo every weekend.

○ boring   ○ fascinating   ○ small   ○ exhausting   ○ uninteresting

12   Last night's full moon was ____, and it was the largest I had ever seen.

○ immense   ○ average   ○ standard   ○ dim   ○ narrow

13   The size of the Vatican, the world's smallest nation is ____ compared to
Russia, the world's largest nation.

○ minuscule   ○ enclosed   ○ patriotic   ○ funny   ○ monumental

14   ____ art museums contain art from recent years.

○ Ancient   ○ Roman   ○ Modern   ○ Antique   ○ Prehistoric

15   The ____ leader went to jail because he had stolen money and lied to the
police.

○ trustworthy   ○ genuine   ○ direct   ○ popular   ○ unethical

16   During the battle, the army fought against their ____.

○ teammate   ○ rival   ○ partner   ○ friend   ○ tank

17   The ____ manager will only be here a short time until our manager can
return to work.

○ permanent   ○ presidential   ○ constant   ○ temporary   ○ obvious

18   Water is a ____ resource because there is a lack of drinking water in some
        parts of the world.

        ○ scarce   ○ damp   ○ humid   ○ huge   ○ amazing

19   Because the car was ____ with water for hours during the flood, it would
        not start.

        ○ washed   ○ sprinkled   ○ cleaned   ○ rained   ○ covered

20   There is not a ____ difference between the two choices, so it does not
        matter to me which one you select.

        ○ perfect   ○ choice   ○ significant   ○ famous   ○ different

21   The man glanced down at his phone and did not see the approaching car,
        causing a ____.

        ○ race   ○ break   ○ competition   ○ rush   ○ collision

22   The view of the vast desert and deep canyons made for an
        incredible ____.

        ○ forest   ○ landscape   ○ swamp   ○ woodland   ○ jungle

HELP MAX FIGURE OUT WHAT'S MISSING.

Directions
(Read these out loud to your child. (S)he may read along silently.)
Look at the top set of pictures. Try to figure out how they belong together. Next, look at the picture on the bottom. The answer is missing. Figure out which answer choice would make the bottom set of pictures go together in the same way that the top set goes together.

Parent note: Use the same methodology to complete Figure Analogies as you used for Verbal Analogies. Work through these together so your child sees how the first set is related. Together, come up with a "rule" to describe how the first set is related. Then, in the second set, look at the first picture. Take this "rule," use it together with the first picture, and figure out which of the answer choices would follow that same rule. For answer choices that do not follow this rule, eliminate them. If your child finds that more than one choice follows this rule, then try to come up with a rule that is more specific.

Example (#1): In the top left box the picture shows a light blue square with four smaller shapes (circles) around it. In the top right box, the picture shows the square, but now the four smaller shapes are inside. These four smaller shapes look the same (size, design) as they did outside the square. The bottom left box shows a light blue square with four smaller shapes (squares) around it. Which answer choice would go with this picture in the same way the top set goes together? Choice C. In Choice C, the four smaller shapes look the same, but now they are inside the square.

1

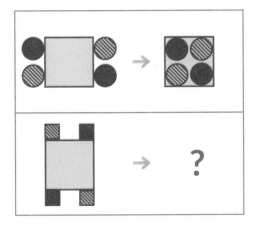

2

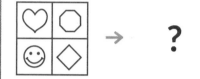

○　　○　　○　　○　　○

3

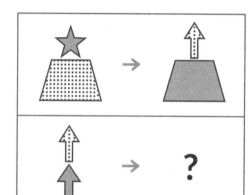

○　　○　　○　　○　　○

4

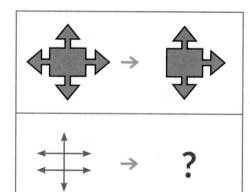

○　　○　　○　　○　　○

5

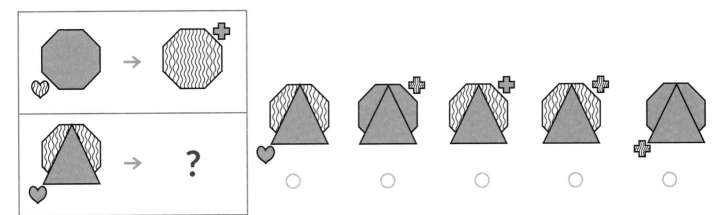

6

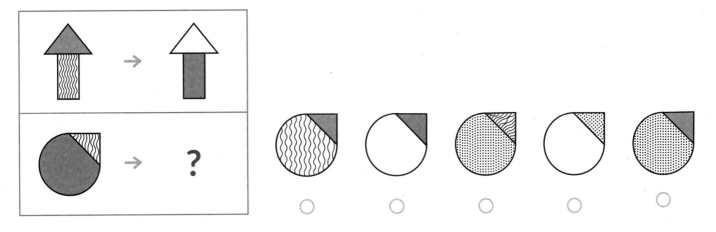

7

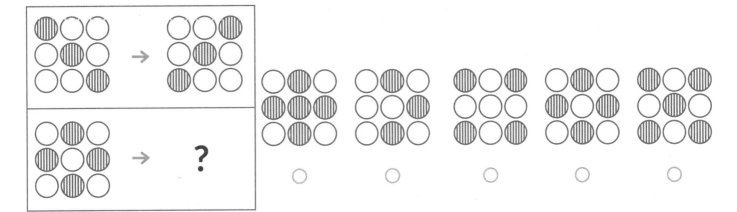

8

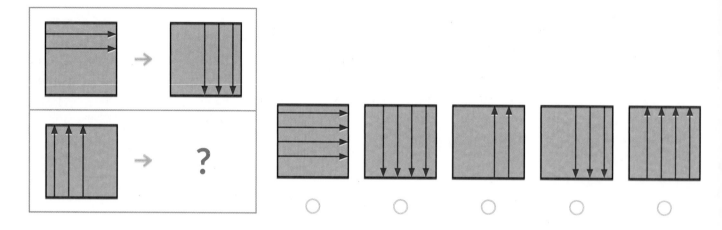

9

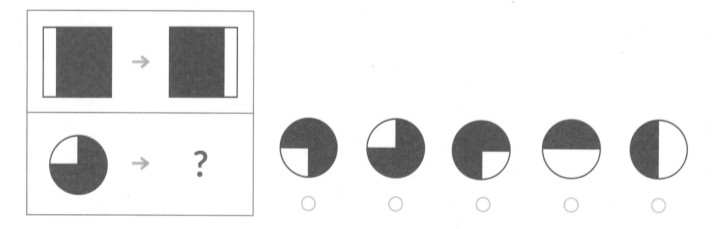

10

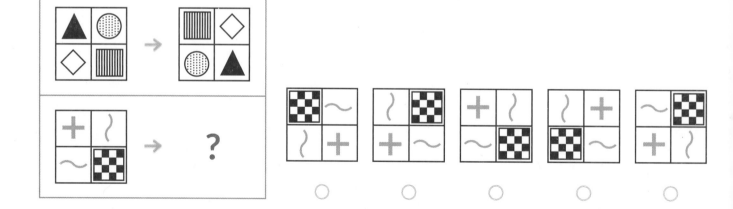

11

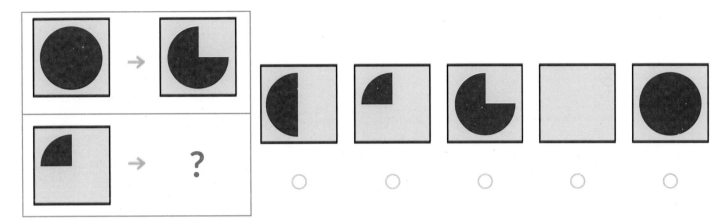

12

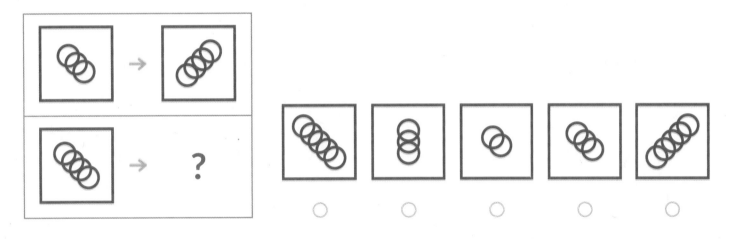

13

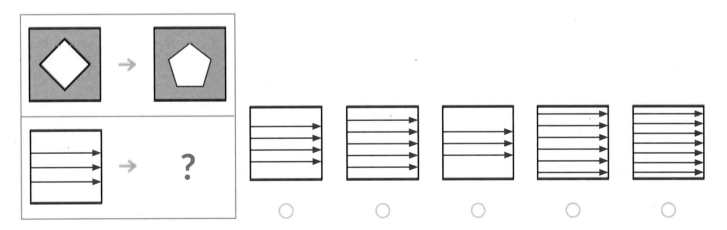

14

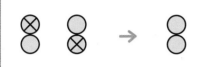

 → ?

○   ○   ○   ○   ○

15

 → ?

○   ○   ○   ○   ○

16

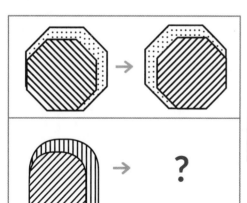 → ?

   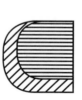  

○   ○   ○   ○   ○

17

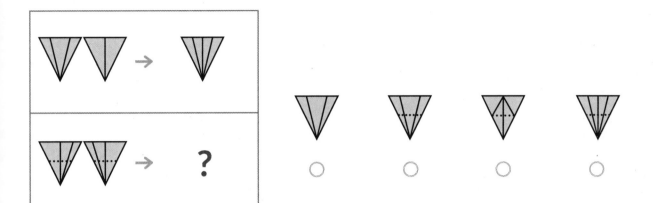

18

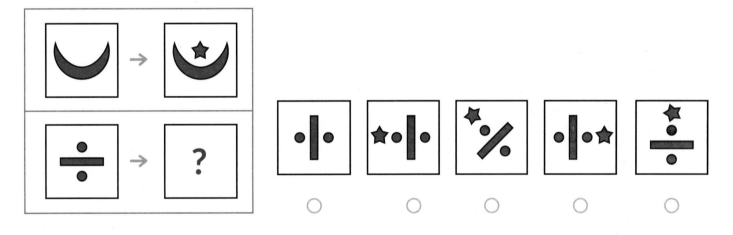

19

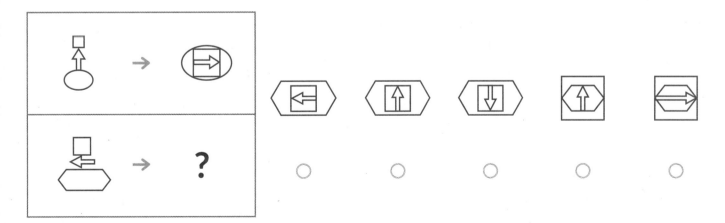

HELP MAY FIGURE OUT WHICH PICTURE BELONGS WITH THE GROUP!

Directions
(Read these out loud to your child. (S)he may read along silently.)
Look at the three pictures on the top row. Figure out how the pictures are alike. Next, look at the pictures in the row of answer choices. Which picture goes best with the three pictures in the top row?

Parent note: As you did with Figure Analogies questions, together, try to come up with a "rule" to describe how the top pictures are alike and go together. Then, take this "rule," and figure out which of the answer choices would best follow that same rule. If your child finds that more than one choice follows the rule, then (s)he should try to come up with a rule that is more specific.

Example (#1): How do these 3 shapes go together? There are 2 parallelograms and 1 oval. What is a rule that describes how they go together? These are light-colored (light purple). Which of the answer choices would follow this rule? The light purple circle.

1

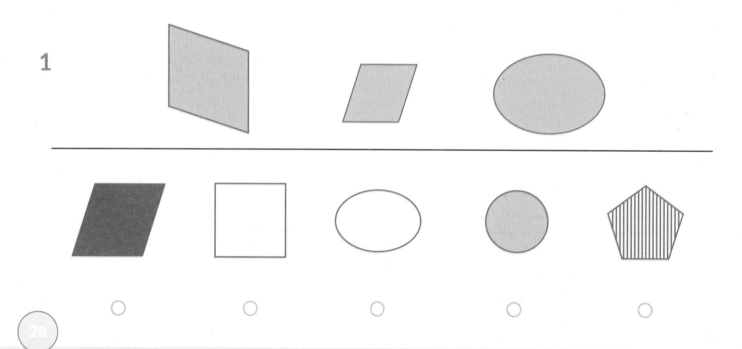

2

    ○   ○   ○   ○

3

       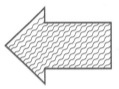

        ○   ○

4

      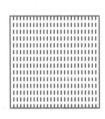

○   ○

5

6

7

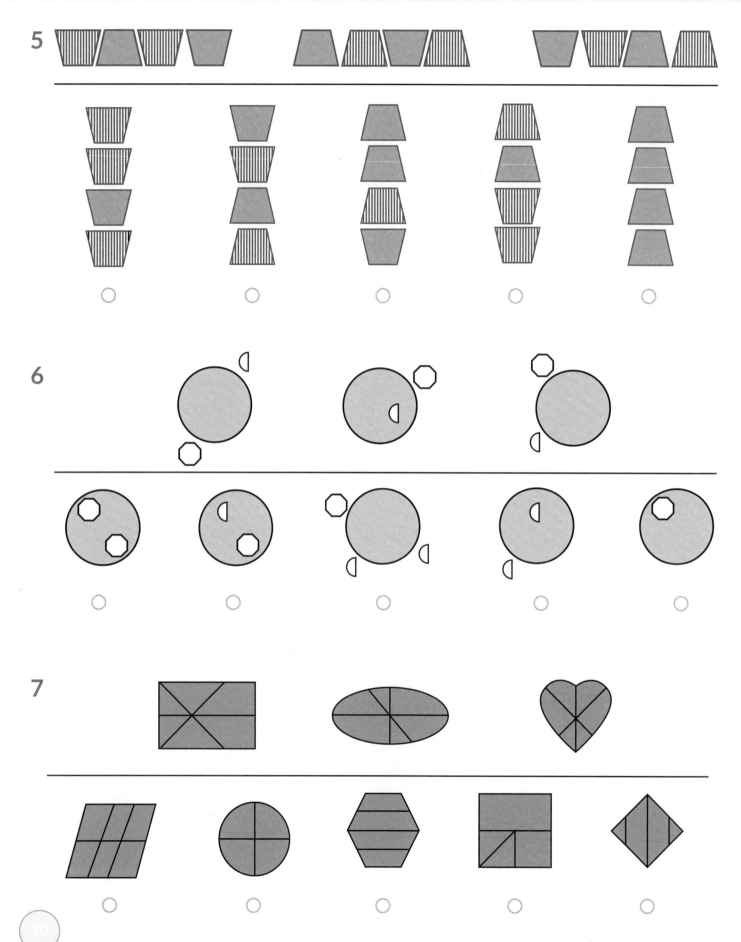

8

○   ○   ○   ○   ○

9

○   ○   ○   ○   ○

10

○   ○   ○   ○   ○

11

12

13

 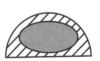

14

☆	☆	♡
☆	♡	♡
♡	♡	☆

☆	♡	☆
♡	♡	♡
☆	☆	☆

♡	☆	♡
☆	♡	☆
♡	☆	♡

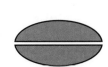

☆	♡	☆
♡	♡	☆
☆	♡	♡

♡	☆	☆
☆	☆	♡
♡	☆	♡

☆	♡	☆
♡	☆	♡
☆	♡	☆

☆	♡	♡
♡	☆	☆
☆	♡	☆

          ○   ○

15

          ▲   ▲   ▱

○   ○   ○   ○   ○

16

     ♡   ○   ◗

○   ○   ○   ○   ○

17

○   ○   ○   ○   ○

18

○   ○   ○   ○   ○

KEEP UP
THE
GOOD
WORK!

LET'S GIVE MAY A HAND!

Directions

(Read these out loud to your child. (S)he child may read along silently.)
The top row of pictures shows a sheet of paper, how it was folded, and then how holes were made in it. Which picture on the bottom row shows how the paper would look after it is unfolded?

Parent note: To help your child better understand, you may wish demonstrate using real paper and a hole puncher (or scissors). Be sure to point out the hole placement and the number of holes made in the paper.

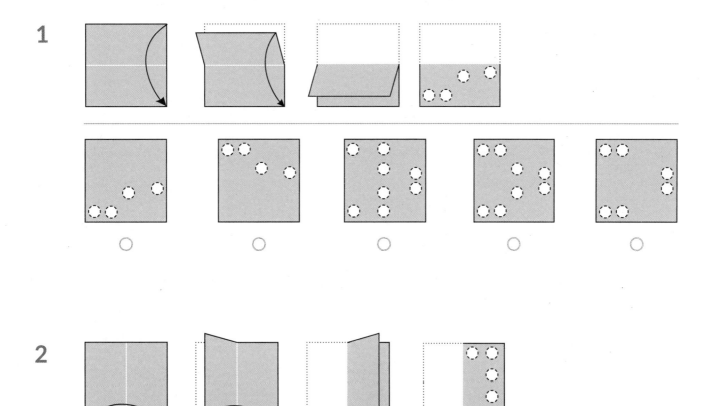

Parent note: Point out that #3-#5 are folded twice. Also, point out the direction of the triangles on #4, #5, and #7.

3

4

5

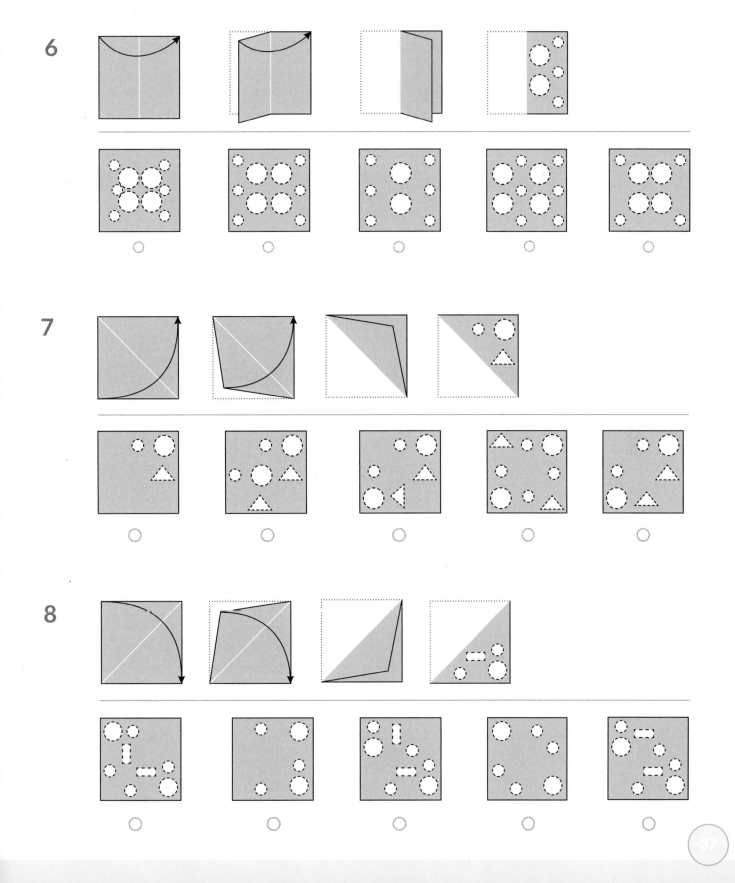

Parent note: Some Paper Folding questions include images of scissors (below). This is simply to show that scissors were used to cut out the shapes.

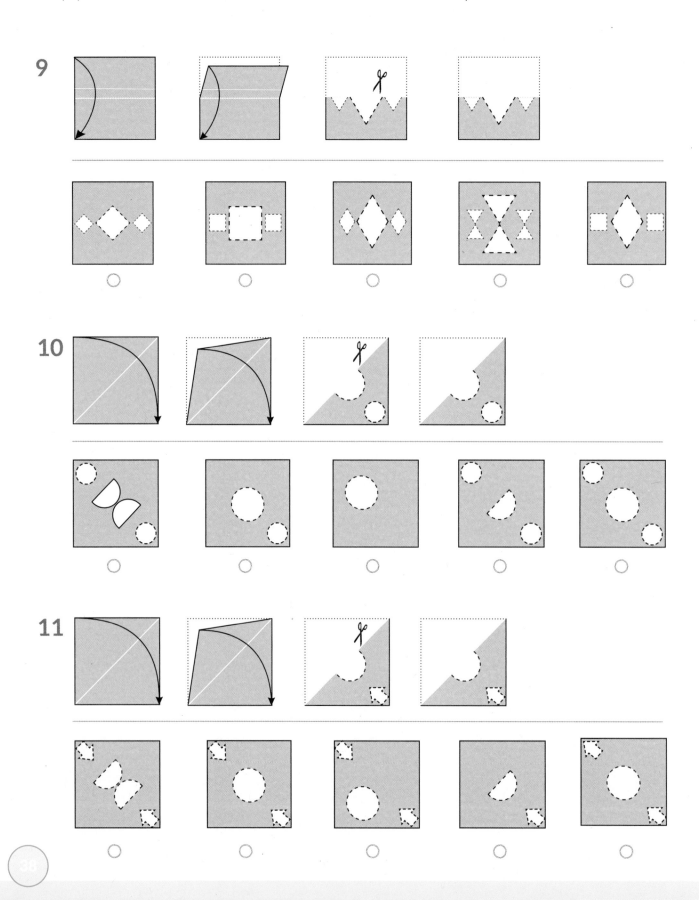

Parent note: Point out that #12 through #16 are folded twice. Also, point out the direction the shapes are facing in #14 through #16.

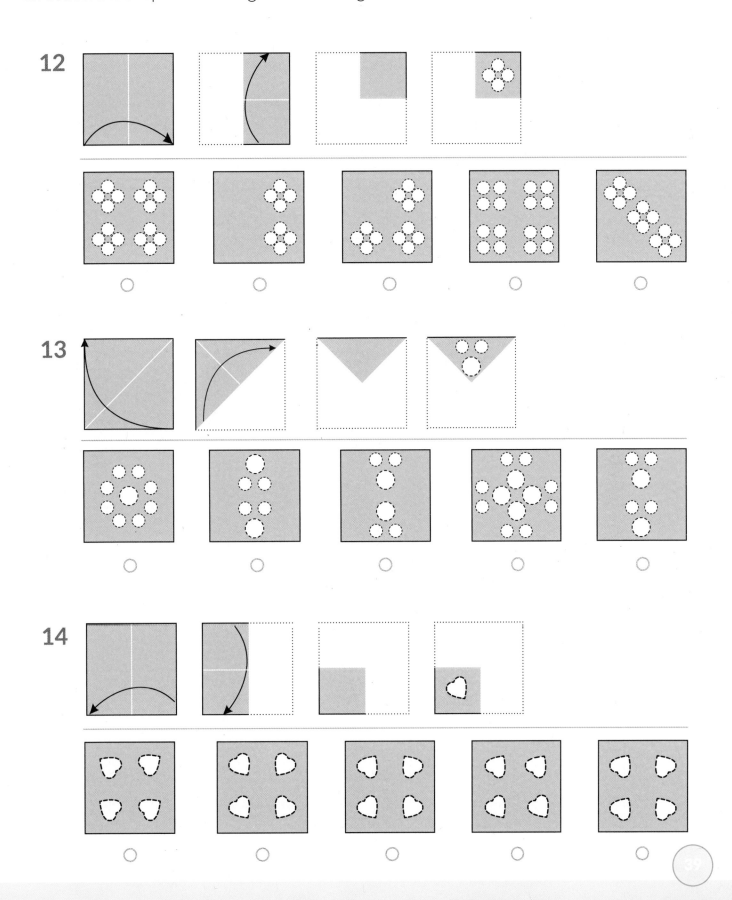

15

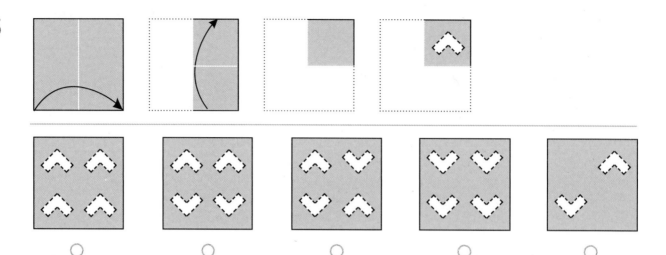

○   ○   ○   ○   ○

16

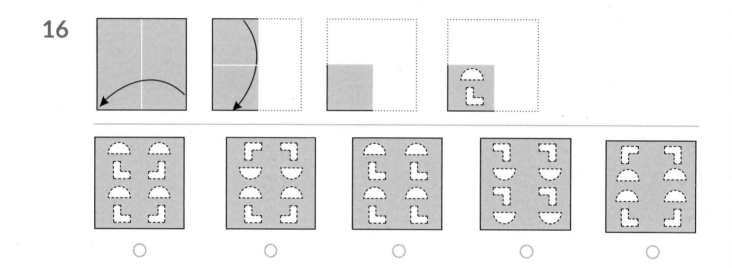

○   ○   ○   ○   ○

17

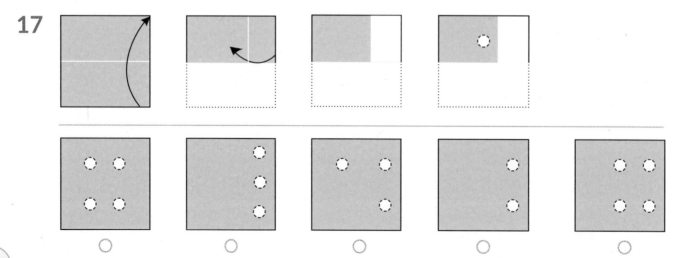

○   ○   ○   ○   ○

LET'S HELP DAVID WITH SOME MATH QUESTIONS!

Directions
(Read these out loud to your child. Your child may read along silently.) What answer choice should you put in the place of the question mark so that both sides of the equal sign total the same amount?

Example: The left side of the equal sign totals 15. Which answer choice do you need to put in the place of the question mark so that the right side of the equal sign totals 15? 33 minus what number equals 15? 33 minus 18 equals 15. So, the answer is 18.

1

$$15 = 33 - \boxed{?}$$

○ 28   ○ 12   ○ 18   ○ 15   ○ 48

2

$$\boxed{?} = \blacklozenge - 2$$
$$\blacklozenge = 24$$

○ 48   ○ 18   ○ 26   ○ 20   ○ 22

3

$$20 + 17 = 40 - \boxed{?}$$

○ 10   ○ 20   ○ 23   ○ 3   ○ 13

4

$$39 = 47 - 3 - \boxed{?}$$

○ 3   ○ 4   ○ 5   ○ 14   ○ 15

5

$$28 = 40 - 19 + \boxed{?}$$

○ 7   ○ 6   ○ 17   ○ 31   ○ 21

6

$$86 = 42 + 25 + \boxed{?}$$

○ 29   ○ 19   ○ 28   ○ 91   ○ 18

7

$$72 - 14 = 60 - \boxed{?}$$

○ 1   ○ 2   ○ 4   ○ 12   ○ 26

8

$$19 + 29 = 65 - \boxed{?}$$

○ 48   ○ 55   ○ 7   ○ 17   ○ 27

9

$$77 = 64 - 9 + \boxed{?}$$

○ 22   ○ 45   ○ 55   ○ 12   ○ 68

10

$$\boxed{?} = \blacklozenge + 59$$
$$\blacklozenge = 23$$

○ 63   ○ 72   ○ 36   ○ 92   ○ 82

11

$$\boxed{?} = \blacklozenge \times 9$$
$$\blacklozenge = 4$$

○ 13   ○ 36   ○ 27   ○ 32   ○ 5

12

$$\boxed{?} = \blacklozenge / 3$$
$$\blacklozenge = 12$$

○ 9   ○ 6   ○ 15   ○ 4   ○ 36

13

$$? = \blacklozenge \times 5$$
$$\blacklozenge = 3$$

◯ 2   ◯ 8   ◯ 15   ◯ 25   ◯ 20

14

$$? = \blacklozenge / 2$$
$$\blacklozenge = 30$$

◯ 16   ◯ 32   ◯ 15   ◯ 28   ◯ 10

15

$$? = \blacklozenge + 28 - 19$$
$$\blacklozenge = 12$$

◯ 21   ◯ 11   ◯ 59   ◯ 49   ◯ 31

16

$$? = \blacklozenge + 41 + 26$$
$$\blacklozenge = 3$$

◯ 21   ◯ 70   ◯ 67   ◯ 18   ◯ 60

17

$$? = \blacklozenge - 31 - 17$$
$$\blacklozenge = 58$$

◯ 24   ◯ 20   ◯ 14   ◯ 30   ◯ 10

WILL YOU HELP MAX WITH MATH QUESTIONS?

Directions

(Read these out loud to your child. Your child may read along silently.) Look at the first two sets of numbers. Come up with a rule that both of these sets follow. Take this rule to figure out which answer choice goes in the place of the question mark.

Parent note: Some questions are in the form of #1 (3 sets aligned vertically with boxes around the numbers), while some are in the form of #2 (3 sets aligned horizontally with no boxes). As with Verbal Analogies, your child must try to come up with a "rule" to answer the question.

Example #1: In the first two sets you have 6 and 5, 4 and 3. How would you get from 6 to 5? How would you get from 4 to 3? In each, you subtract 1 from the first number. This is the "rule". Take this rule and apply it to the bottom set. What is the answer when you subtract 1 from 2? The answer is 1.

Example #2: In the first two sets, you have 10 and 5, 8 and 4. How would you get from 10 to 5? How would you get from 8 to 4? In each, you must divide the first number in half. Or, you must divide by 2. This is the "rule". Take this rule and apply it to the last set. What is the answer when you divide 6 by 2? The answer is 3.

1

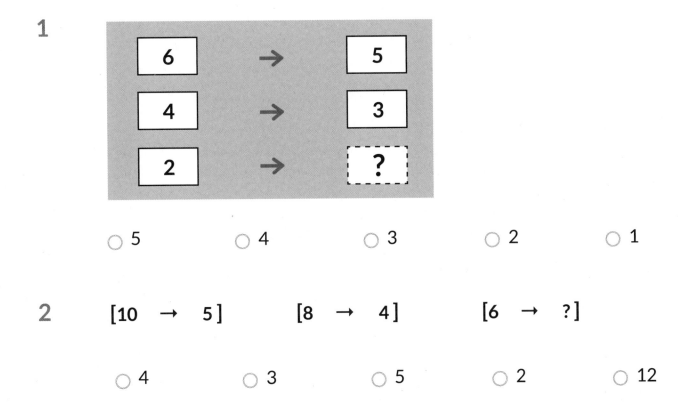

    ○ 5   ○ 4   ○ 3   ○ 2   ○ 1

2   [10 → 5]   [8 → 4]   [6 → ?]

    ○ 4   ○ 3   ○ 5   ○ 2   ○ 12

3

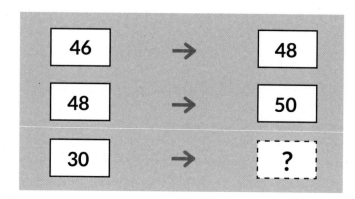

46 → 48	
48 → 50	
30 → ?	

○ 34　　　○ 28　　　○ 42　　　○ 32　　　○ 52

4

6 → 18	
20 → 60	
7 → ?	

○ 21　　　○ 10　　　○ 14　　　○ 13　　　○ 3

5

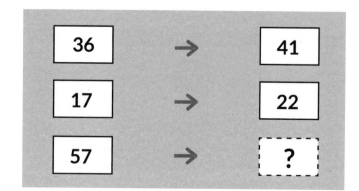

36 → 41	
17 → 22	
57 → ?	

○ 55　　　○ 62　　　○ 52　　　○ 27　　　○ 15

6

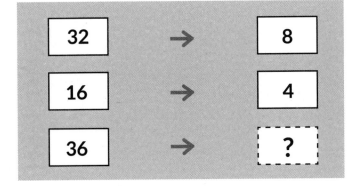

- ○ 4
- ○ 9
- ○ 32
- ○ 40
- ○ 7

7

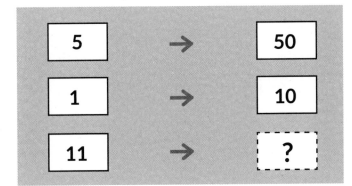

- ○ 90
- ○ 10
- ○ 110
- ○ 21
- ○ 100

8

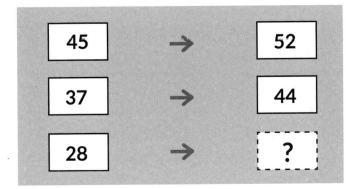

- ○ 35
- ○ 37
- ○ 25
- ○ 21
- ○ 31

9   [6 → 12]   [9 → 18]   [11 → ?]

○ 20   ○ 17   ○ 22   ○ 24   ○ 2

10   [32 → 23]   [45 → 36]   [50 → ?]

○ 51   ○ 31   ○ 59   ○ 41   ○ 56

11   [41 → 34]   [29 → 22]   [44 → ?]

○ 47   ○ 22   ○ 32   ○ 51   ○ 37

12   [29 → 33]   [37 → 41]   [51 → ?]

○ 37   ○ 44   ○ 47   ○ 55   ○ 54

13   [30 → 27]   [18 → 15]   [42 → ?]

○ 18   ○ 38   ○ 40   ○ 45   ○ 39

14   [6 → 30]   [5 → 25]   [7 → ?]

    ○ 35   ○ 30   ○ 5   ○ 12   ○ 20

15   [43 → 52]   [41 → 50]   [42 → ?]

    ○ 33   ○ 31   ○ 59   ○ 51   ○ 45

16   [30 → 10]   [18 → 6]   [24 → ?]

    ○ 9   ○ 27   ○ 8   ○ 12   ○ 7

17   [29 → 24]   [31 → 26]   [52 → ?]

    ○ 21   ○ 57   ○ 47   ○ 5   ○ 29

18   [22 → 11]   [18 → 9]   [12 → ?]

    ○ 8   ○ 6   ○ 10   ○ 14   ○ 20

GREAT WORK. WE ARE ALMOST DONE!

Directions

(Read these out loud to your child. Your child may read along silently.) Here, you must try to figure out a pattern that the numbers have made. Which answer choice would complete the pattern?

Parent note: Some questions are in the form of #1 (an abacus), while some are in the form of #2 (a series of numbers).

Example #1: Here is an abacus. The rods have made a pattern. Below the rods is the number of beads it has. 8 beads, 7 beads, 6 beads, 5 beads. Here we see that the number of beads decreases by 1 each time. Then, after 5 beads, there are 6 beads. Here, the number of beads starts increasing by 1 each time. What comes after 6 beads? It's choice D, 7 beads.

Example #2: Do you see a pattern or a rule that the numbers in the series follow? Each time, each number increases by 2. If this is the pattern, then what would come after 20? It's Choice E, 22.

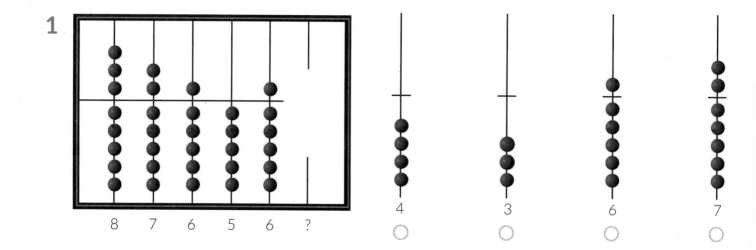

1

8   7   6   5   6   ?

4   3   6   7
○   ○   ○   ○

2   10   12   14   16   18   20   ?

○ 20   ○ 24   ○ 2   ○ 21   ○ 22

3

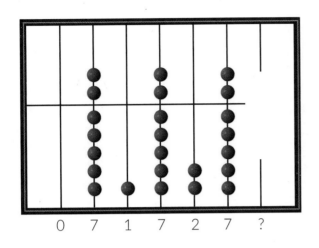

0   7   1   7   2   7   ?

0
○

7
○

5
○

3
○

4

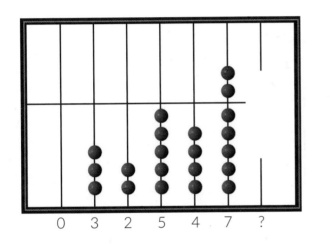

0   3   2   5   4   7   ?

2
○

3
○

4
○

6
○

5

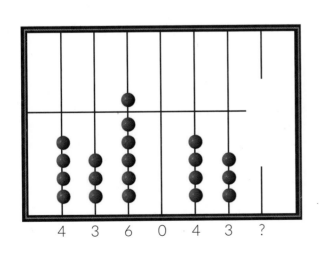

4   3   6   0   4   3   ?

6
○

5
○

4
○

3
○

6

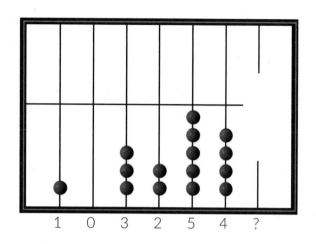

1　0　3　2　5　4　?

6　　4　　7　　3
○　　○　　○　　○

7

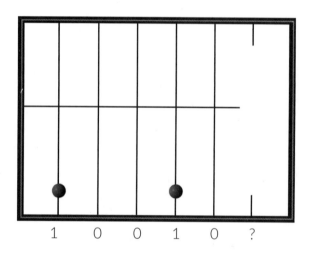

1　0　0　1　0　?

0　　1　　2　　3
○　　○　　○　　○

8

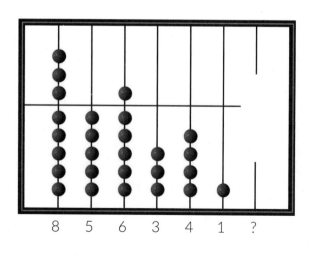

8　5　6　3　4　1　?

0　　2　　4　　5
○　　○　　○　　○

9   **41**   **36**   **31**   **26**   **21**   **16**   **?**

    ○ 11   ○ 15   ○ 5   ○ 31   ○ 32

10   **3**   **4**   **6**   **7**   **9**   **10**   **?**

    ○ 13   ○ 12   ○ 10   ○ 8   ○ 9

11   **20**   **19**   **17**   **16**   **14**   **13**   **?**

    ○ 12   ○ 13   ○ 10   ○ 11   ○ 26

12   **6**   **8**   **12**   **14**   **18**   **20**   **?**

    ○ 28   ○ 14   ○ 26   ○ 24   ○ 22

13   **20**   **23**   **19**   **22**   **18**   **21**   **?**

    ○ 24   ○ 16   ○ 17   ○ 16   ○ 25

14   **43**   **46**   **46**   **49**   **49**   **52**   **?**

   ○ 52   ○ 55   ○ 47   ○ 48   ○ 51

15   **1.5**   **2.5**   **3.5**   **4.5**   **5.5**   **6.5**   **?**

   ○ 7.6   ○ 6.6   ○ 5.6   ○ 7.0   ○ 7.5

16   **0.05**   **0.10**   **0.15**   **0.20**   **0.25**   **0.30**   **?**

   ○ 0.55   ○ 0.20   ○ 3.50   ○ 0.35   ○ 0.33

17   **64**   **63**   **62**   **60**   **59**   **58**   **?**

   ○ 65   ○ 60   ○ 55   ○ 58   ○ 56

18   **53**   **62**   **71**   **80**   **89**   **98**   **?**

   ○ 91   ○ 107   ○ 90   ○ 99   ○ 109

19   **1.0**   **2.5**   **4.0**   **5.5**   **7.0**   **8.5**   **?**

   ○ 9.0   ○ 8.0   ○ 10.0   ○ 9.5   ○ 10.5

PRACTICE TEST 2
BEGINS ON THE NEXT PAGE

PRACTICE TEST 2 NOTES

- Our suggestion: have your child complete Practice Test 2 on his/her own
  (do not tell your child whether answers are correct or not until the test is completed - see below).

- You read the directions to your child while your child reads along silently if they wish.

- The time limit for each of the 9 question sections (Verbal Analogies, Verbal Classification, etc.) is approximately 10 minutes each.

Our suggestion: do a group of 3 question sections per day.
- Day 1, Verbal: 10 minutes each for Verbal Analogies, Verbal Classification, Sentence Completion = 30 minutes total
- Day 2, Non-Verbal: 10 minutes each for Figure Analogies, Figure Classification, Paper Folding = 30 minutes total
- Day 3, Quantitative: 10 minutes each for Number Analogies, Number Puzzles, Number Series = 30 minutes total

- After your child is done, on your own (without your child) go through the answer key by question type. Write the number answered correctly in the space provided on the Answer Key (page 94).

- This is not meant to be used as an official assessment, but it will give a general overview of strengths/weaknesses, by question type.

- For questions answered incorrectly, go over the question and answer choices again with him/her.

- Compare the answer choices, specifically what the question is asking and what makes the correct answer choice the right choice.

We offer additional COGAT® practice books as well as FREE COGAT® Level 9 quantitative questions in eBook format.

See page 96 and get your free eBook today!

Directions: Which choice makes the second set of words go together in the same way the first set does?

1   mechanic → engine : plumber →

     ○ truck   ○ fan   ○ drain   ○ roof   ○ wrench

2   push → pull : south →

     ○ up   ○ west   ○ east   ○ southern   ○ north

3   river → creek : cavern →

     ○ cave   ○ cliff   ○ rock   ○ boulder   ○ hike

4   hair → fur : foot →

     ○ ear   ○ animal   ○ claw   ○ paw   ○ hand

5   bear → growl: snake →

     ○ roar   ○ hiss   ○ bite   ○ poison   ○ chirp

6   Europe → Atlantic : Asia →

     ○ Persian Gulf   ○ Baltic   ○ Pacific   ○ China   ○ Suez Canal

7   pool → loop : trams →

     ○ book   ○ smart   ○ train   ○ circle   ○ lambs

8   ruler → length : compass →

     ○ direction   ○ west   ○ trip   ○ area   ○ map

9   house → attic : mountain →

     ○ hike   ○ snow   ○ rocks   ○ peak   ○ trail

10   peacock → owl : shark →

     ○ tuna   ○ crab   ○ pelican   ○ octopus   ○ coral

11   weight → pound : temperature →

○ thermometer   ○ number   ○ degree   ○ heat   ○ season

12   innocent → guilty : success →

○ succeed   ○ failure   ○ practice   ○ incorrect   ○ ruin

13   hand → feel : mouth →

○ cook   ○ food   ○ digest   ○ swallow   ○ taste

14   Russia → Brazil : China →

○ New York   ○ Africa   ○ London   ○ Atlantic   ○ France

15   lettuce → vegetable : acorn →

○ almond   ○ bean   ○ nut   ○ peanut   ○ shell

16   monkey → horse : turtle →

○ bat   ○ lizard   ○ snail   ○ rabbit   ○ seagull

17   carriage → car : bicycle →

○ wagon   ○ skateboard   ○ tricycle   ○ unicycle   ○ motorcycle

18   saw → chainsaw : screwdriver →

○ ruler   ○ hammer   ○ wrench   ○ drill   ○ nail

19   bread → grain : paper →

○ tree   ○ book   ○ pencil   ○ notebook   ○ sheet

20   twins → pair : triplets →

○ triangle   ○ trio   ○ double   ○ match   ○ couple

Directions: The top 3 words go together in some way. Which answer choice goes best with the top words?

1   yellow   gray   purple

○ paints   ○ mix   ○ crayons   ○ pink   ○ colors

2   house   castle   igloo

○ station   ○ bus stop   ○ roof   ○ airport   ○ apartment

3   English   French   Russian

○ Italian   ○ China   ○ Ireland   ○ Europe   ○ Panama

4   seeing   smelling   hearing

○ sleeping   ○ opening   ○ tasting   ○ closing   ○ waiting

5   scale   compass   speedometer

○ speed   ○ directions   ○ north   ○ weight   ○ ruler

6   helmet   cap   bonnet

○ sweater   ○ hat   ○ glove   ○ tie   ○ jacket

7   ladder   elevator   staircase

○ trampoline   ○ jump   ○ escalator   ○ cage   ○ see-saw

8   sun   seahorse   sweater

○ acorn   ○ boot   ○ water   ○ moon   ○ six

9   fork   knife   chopsticks

○ glass   ○ bowl   ○ plate   ○ spoon   ○ cup

10   Pacific   Indian   Arctic

○ Greenland   ○ Caribbean   ○ Atlantic   ○ North Sea   ○ Persian Gulf

11   **street**   **driveway**   **alley**

○ highway   ○ river   ○ train tracks   ○ concrete   ○ stoplight

12   **cheerful**   **glad**   **joyful**

○ worried   ○ shocked   ○ delighted   ○ concerned   ○ smile

13   **socks**   **dice**   **skis**

○ fruit   ○ fish   ○ jackets   ○ gloves   ○ scarves

14   **raccoon**   **rabbit**   **rhinoceros**

○ chicken   ○ horse   ○ reptile   ○ robin   ○ rattlesnake

15   **pine tree**   **cactus**   **grass**

○ cedar tree   ○ algae   ○ coral   ○ bouquet   ○ stick

16   **drowsy**   **sleepy**   **exhausted**

○ bed   ○ awake   ○ energy   ○ nap   ○ tired

17   **hourglass**   **stopwatch**   **sundial**

○ calculator   ○ scale   ○ clock   ○ alphabet   ○ code

18   **scissors**   **lawn mower**   **knife**

○ bread   ○ paper   ○ razor   ○ sharp   ○ straw

19   **water**   **milk**   **gasoline**

○ vinegar   ○ wood   ○ sand   ○ cotton   ○ helium

20   **turtle**   **armadillo**   **crab**

○ goldfish   ○ rooster   ○ mouse   ○ snail   ○ frog

Directions: There is a missing word in the sentence. Which answer choice would go best in the sentence?

1 **She was so ____ while building her sand castle, she did not notice her beach towel blowing away in the wind.**

   ○ lazy   ○ focused   ○ aware   ○ watchful   ○ alert

2 **The temperature will ____ little here, so you hardly notice a change in seasons.**

   ○ stay   ○ predict   ○ remain   ○ vary   ○ measure

3 **The hexagons of honeycombs, along with the arcs and circles of rainbows, are a few examples of ____ found in nature.**

   ○ games   ○ jokes   ○ astronomy   ○ subtraction ○ geometry

4 **I experienced a memory ____ and could not recall my teacher's name.**

   ○ loss   ○ recovery   ○ concentration   ○ time   ○ renewal

5 **Blueberries are healthy because they are high in ____ including Vitamin C and fiber.**

   ○ sugars   ○ juices   ○ nutrients   ○ foods   ○ letters

6   When a bank loans someone money, that person must ____ some of the loan each month until no more money is owed.

○ repay   ○ lend   ○ spend   ○ check   ○ borrow

7   Jeff prefers peaceful country life to city life, which he finds too ____.

○ large   ○ hectic   ○ quiet   ○ relaxed   ○ gentle

8   The Alps mountains serve as a natural ____ separating France from Italy.

○ trail   ○ law   ○ language   ○ border   ○ country

9   We were ____ because we spent hours waiting in line to enter the water park, only to discover the park had already reached its visitor limit.

○ excited   ○ ready   ○ eager   ○ welcoming   ○ furious

10   As a ____ club, membership is not given to all who wish to join.

○ private   ○ crowded   ○ public   ○ free   ○ open

11 Viewing the eclipse was such an ____ experience, it was more than anything I had expected.

○ expected   ○ imagined   ○ ordinary   ○ acceptable   ○ astonishing

12 In World War II, some countries had to ____ food to ensure people did not starve.

○ destroy   ○ ration   ○ damage   ○ battle   ○ ruin

13 Camels can ____ long trips through deserts, because they can store fat, a source of energy, in their humps.

○ fail   ○ decrease   ○ complete   ○ pause   ○ reduce

14 When my sister creates ____ pictures, it's impossible for me to understand what she has painted.

○ actual   ○ frame   ○ clear   ○ abstract   ○ precise

15 I am a ____ of George Washington, my most famous ancestor.

○ forefather   ○ descendant   ○ elder   ○ mentor   ○ sibling

16   Our change of schools was ____, and we will not return to our previous school
      again.

      ○ educational ○ short   ○ temporary ○ permanent ○ acting

17   The apartment building has been ____ for two years because no one wants
      to live there.

      ○ full   ○ vacant   ○ packed   ○ comfortable ○ tall

18   The hospital's waiting room and the doctor's office are ____, so we will not
      have to walk far once the nurse calls our name.

      ○ remote   ○ abroad   ○ inaccessible ○ distant   ○ connected

19   My parents must sign this ____ form which shows that I am allowed to go
      on the field trip.

      ○ vacation   ○ refusal   ○ approval   ○ welcome   ○ return

20   Taking care of the farm has created a ____ for me, because instead of
      playing after school, I must now spend two hours cleaning the barn.

      ○ burden   ○ hobby   ○ relief   ○ solution   ○ favor

Directions: Which choice makes the second set of pictures go together in the same way as the first set?

1

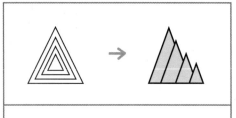

○ ○ ○ ○ ○

2

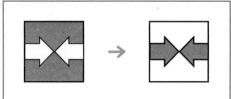

○ ○ ○ ○ ○

3

○ ○ ○ ○ ○

4

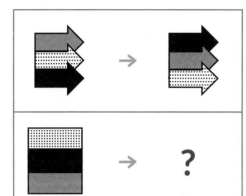

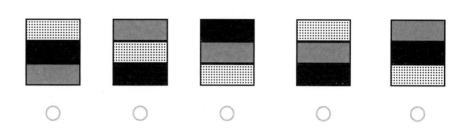

5

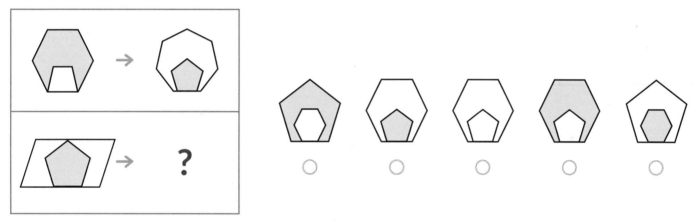

6

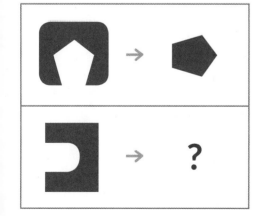

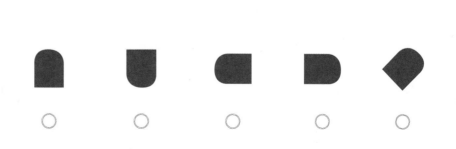

7

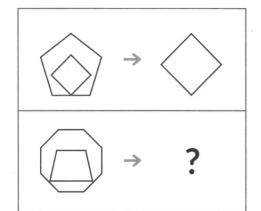

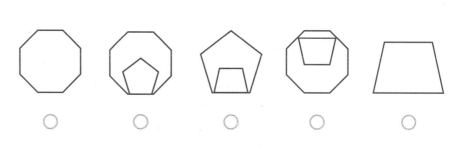

8

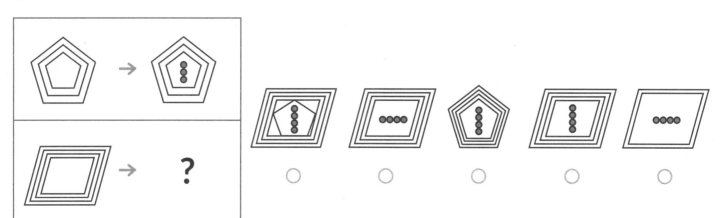

9

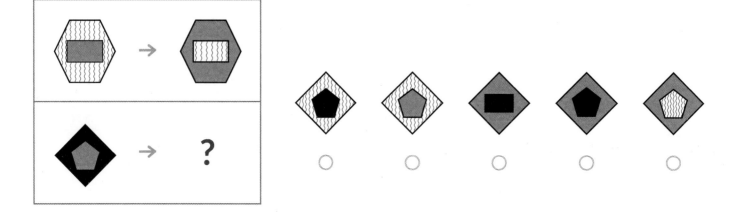

10

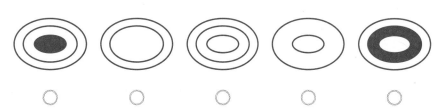

11

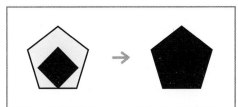

12

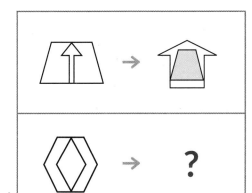

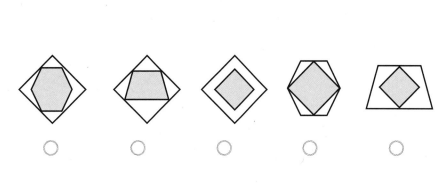

13

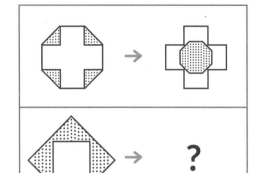

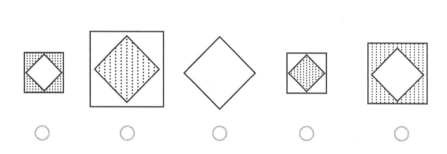

14

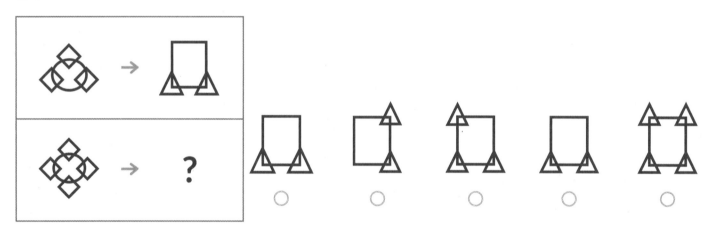

15

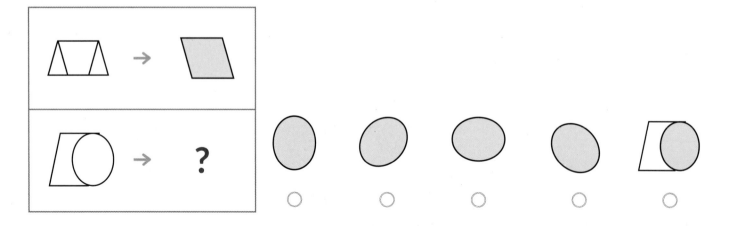

16

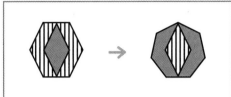

○　　○　　○　　○　　○

17

○　　○　　○　　○　　○

18

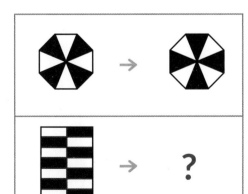
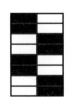
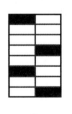
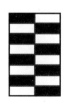
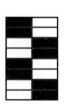
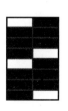

○　　○　　○　　○　　○

Directions: Which answer choice in the bottom row goes best with the 3 pictures in the top row?

1

○　　　○　　　○　　　○　　　○

2

○　　　○　　　○　　　○　　　○

3

○　　　○　　　○　　　○　　　○

4

5

6

7

○   ○   ○   ○   ○

8

○   ○   ○   ○   ○

9

○   ○   ○   ○   ○

10

○   ○   ○   ○   ○

11

 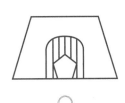   

○   ○   ○   ○   ○

12

  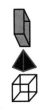

○   ○   ○   ○   ○

13

○   ○   ○   ○   ○

14

○   ○   ○   ○   ○

15

AUW   UWA   WAU

WꓵA   UAW   AWU   MUA   UWA

○   ○   ○   ○   ○

16

                ○

17

○   ○   ○   ○   ○

18

    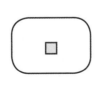   

○   ○   ○   ○   ○

Directions: The top row shows a sheet of paper, how it was folded, and how holes were made in it. Which picture on the bottom row shows how the paper would look unfolded?

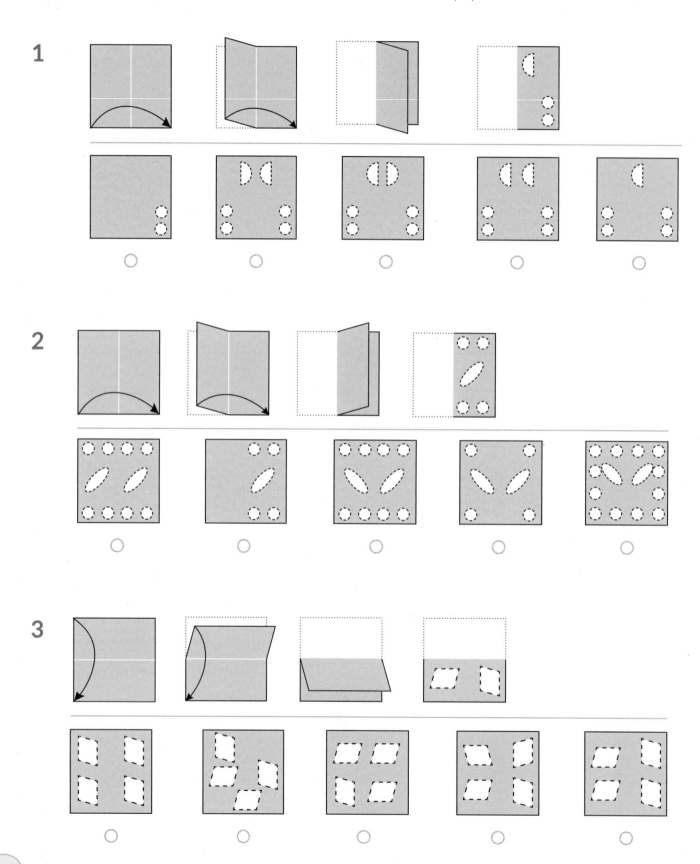

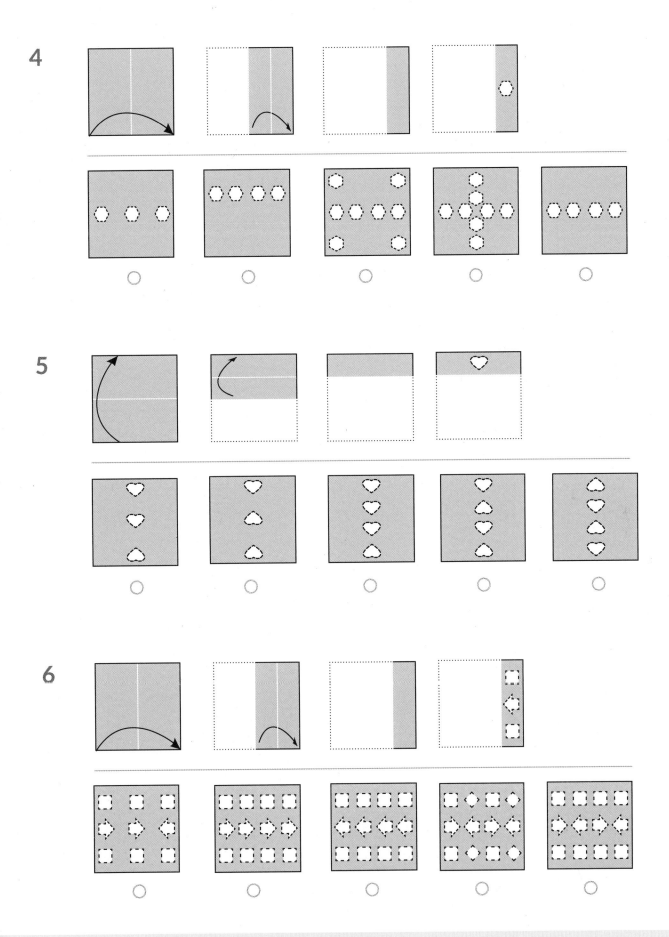

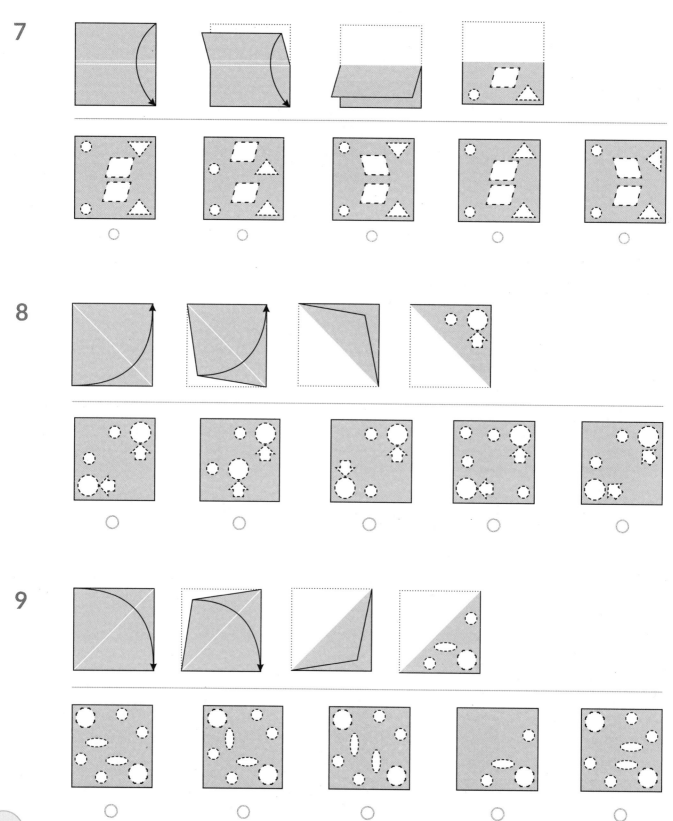

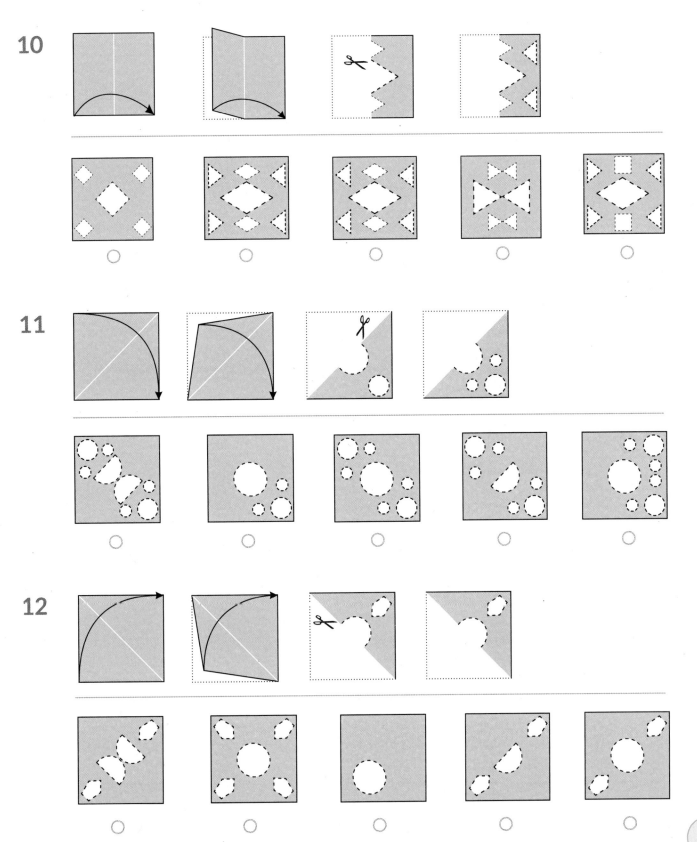

13

14

15

Directions: What answer choice should you put in the place of the question mark so that both sides of the equal sign total the same amount?

1

$$67 = 39 + \boxed{?}$$

○ 28 ○ 18 ○ 38 ○ 105 ○ 32

2

$$40 = 59 - \boxed{?}$$

○ 299 ○ 1 ○ 21 ○ 11 ○ 19

3

$$35 / \boxed{?} = 7$$

○ 6 ○ 5 ○ 4 ○ 3 ○ 42

4

$$9 \ X \ \boxed{?} = 45$$

○ 6 ○ 36 ○ 54 ○ 5 ○ 7

5

$$32 + 33 = 71 - \boxed{?}$$

○ 5 ○ 6 ○ 15 ○ 16 ○ 38

6

$$54 - 25 = 68 - \boxed{?}$$

○ 29   ○ 9   ○ 39   ○ 19   ○ 43

7

$$23 + 19 = 44 - \boxed{?}$$

○ 0   ○ 1   ○ 2   ○ 3   ○ 40

8

$$28 = \boxed{?} \times 7$$

○ 3   ○ 4   ○ 5   ○ 6   ○ 21

9

$$\boxed{?} = \blacklozenge + 37 + 28$$
$$\blacklozenge = 6$$

○ 17   ○ 70   ○ 65   ○ 60   ○ 71

10

$$\boxed{?} = \blacklozenge + 45 - 16$$
$$\blacklozenge = 12$$

○ 31   ○ 41   ○ 14   ○ 21   ○ 29

11   31 + 19 = 71 - [?]

○ 11   ○ 50   ○ 21   ○ 17   ○ 31

12   53 = 68 - 29 + [?]

○ 24   ○ 34   ○ 39   ○ 14   ○ 15

13   [?] = ◆ + 48
          ◆ = 29

○ 77   ○ 67   ○ 48   ○ 29   ○ 87

14   [?] = ◆ x 8
          ◆ = 7

○ 42   ○ 64   ○ 49   ○ 15   ○ 56

15   [?] = ◆ / 7
          ◆ = 21

○ 2   ○ 3   ○ 4   ○ 14   ○ 28

16

$$? = \blacklozenge \times 6$$
$$\blacklozenge = 8$$

○ 14   ○ 2   ○ 56   ○ 48   ○ 40

17

$$? = \blacklozenge / 5$$
$$\blacklozenge = 40$$

○ 15   ○ 45   ○ 8   ○ 35   ○ 7

18

$$? = \blacklozenge + 26 - 33$$
$$\blacklozenge = 54$$

○ 57   ○ 21   ○ 37   ○ 80   ○ 47

19

$$? = \blacklozenge + 19 + 40$$
$$\blacklozenge = 18$$

○ 59   ○ 77   ○ 67   ○ 57   ○ 37

20

$$? = \blacklozenge - 52 - 9$$
$$\blacklozenge = 63$$

○ 1   ○ 2   ○ 11   ○ 43   ○ 21

Directions: Look at the first two sets of numbers. Come up with a rule that both sets follow. Take this rule to figure out which answer choice goes in the place of the question mark.

1

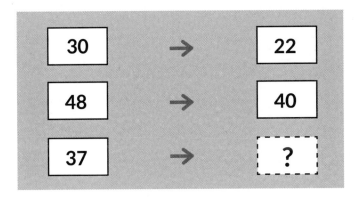

○ 38   ○ 29   ○ 49   ○ 40   ○ 45

2

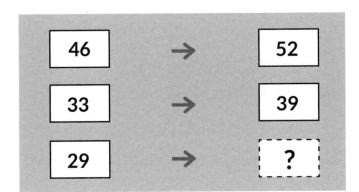

○ 35   ○ 36   ○ 23   ○ 45   ○ 6

3

16	→	26
17	→	27
40	→	?

○ 20   ○ 28   ○ 60   ○ 30   ○ 50

4

9	→	18
8	→	16
11	→	?

○ 9   ○ 13   ○ 22   ○ 20   ○ 24

5

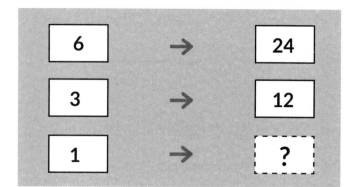

6	→	24
3	→	12
1	→	?

○ 5   ○ 44   ○ 3   ○ 4   ○ 6

6

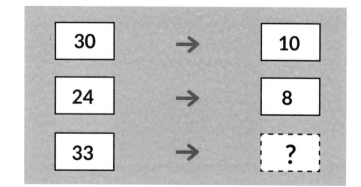

30	→	10
24	→	8
33	→	?

○ 12   ○ 11   ○ 10   ○ 30   ○ 36

7   [22 → 30]   [9 → 17]   [40 → ?]

    ○ 28   ○ 22   ○ 38   ○ 48   ○ 32

8   [40 → 38]   [51 → 49]   [31 → ?]

    ○ 33   ○ 32   ○ 29   ○ 19   ○ 39

9   [35 → 29]   [47 → 41]   [24 → ?]

    ○ 42   ○ 18   ○ 28   ○ 38   ○ 30

10   [3 → 6]   [37 → 40]   [19 → ?]

    ○ 22   ○ 16   ○ 43   ○ 30   ○ 6

11   [21 → 17]   [48 → 44]   [4 → ?]

    ○ 8   ○ 16   ○ 0   ○ 1   ○ 40

12   [51 → 41]   [29 → 19]   [43 → ?]

    ○ 53   ○ 32   ○ 44   ○ 34   ○ 33

13   [7 → 14]   [31 → 38]   [44 → ?]

  ○ 41   ○ 51   ○ 45   ○ 7   ○ 37

14   [38 → 40]   [4 → 6]   [29 → ?]

  ○ 27   ○ 13   ○ 49   ○ 8   ○ 31

15   [40 → 4]   [30 → 3]   [10 → ?]

  ○ 11   ○ 20   ○ 1   ○ 0   ○ 10

16   [8 → 24]   [11 → 33]   [5 → ?]

  ○ 10   ○ 15   ○ 8   ○ 36   ○ 20

17   [4 → 1]   [20 → 5]   [40 → ?]

  ○ 36   ○ 11   ○ 4   ○ 10   ○ 16

18   [25 → 5]   [35 → 7]   [40 → ?]

  ○ 8   ○ 9   ○ 5   ○ 35   ○ 45

Directions: Which answer choice would complete the pattern?

1

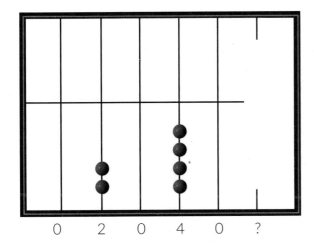

0   2   0   4   0   ?

0   1   5   6
○   ○   ○   ○

2

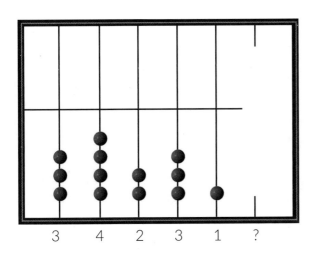

3   4   2   3   1   ?

2   0   3   1
○   ○   ○   ○

3

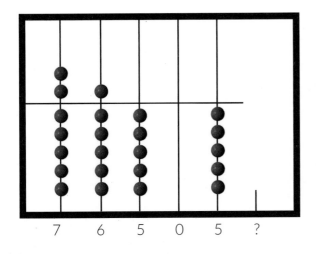

7   6   5   0   5   ?

5   6   3   2
○   ○   ○   ○

89

4

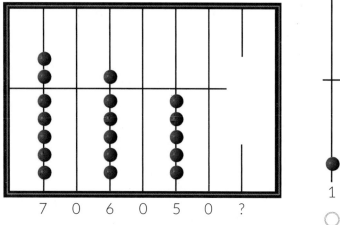

7 0 6 0 5 0 ?

1 ○

3 ○

4 ○

5 ○

5

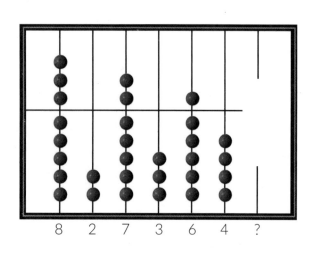

8 2 7 3 6 4 ?

1 ○

3 ○

4 ○

5 ○

6

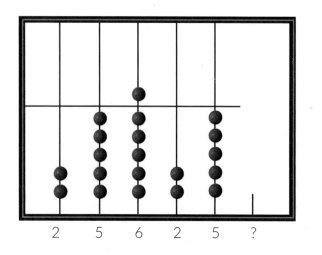

2 5 6 2 5 ?

1 ○

2 ○

3 ○

6 ○

1 **29**   **32**   **35**   **38**   **41**   **44**   **?**

○ 64   ○ 73   ○ 40   ○ 46   ○ 47

2 **10**   **22**   **34**   **46**   **58**   **70**   **?**

○ 82   ○ 72   ○ 80   ○ 84   ○ 56

3 **14**   **16**   **17**   **19**   **20**   **22**   **?**

○ 21   ○ 23   ○ 24   ○ 18   ○ 26

4 **1**   **0**   **1**   **2**   **1**   **4**   **?**

○ 5   ○ 4   ○ 1   ○ 3   ○ 6

5 **76**   **65**   **54**   **43**   **32**   **21**   **?**

○ 31   ○ 9   ○ 12   ○ 11   ○ 10

6 **55**   **55**   **57**   **57**   **59**   **59**   **?**

○ 61   ○ 58   ○ 60   ○ 63   ○ 59

7 **37.5**   **37.0**   **36.5**   **36.0**   **35.5**   **35.0**   **?**

○ 35.0   ○ 34.5   ○ 34.0   ○ 38.5   ○ 34.55

8 **49**   **50**   **58**   **59**   **67**   **68**   **?**

○ 69   ○ 70   ○ 77   ○ 76   ○ 78

9 **4**   **5**   **6**   **8**   **9**   **10**   **?**

○ 13   ○ 8   ○ 14   ○ 11   ○ 12

10 **20.3**   **19.3**   **18.3**   **17.3**   **16.3**   **15.3**   **?**

○ 13.3   ○ 13.5   ○ 14.3   ○ 10.3   ○ 11.3

11 **39**   **49**   **51**   **61**   **63**   **73**   **?**

○ 74   ○ 75   ○ 83   ○ 53   ○ 93

12 **20**   **18**   **21**   **19**   **22**   **20**   **?**

○ 23   ○ 21   ○ 18   ○ 30   ○ 24

- Write your child's answer in the blank space (_____).
- At the end of each group of questions, total the number of questions answered correctly. This will provide a general overview of strengths/weaknesses according to COGAT® question type.

Verbal Analogies, p. 10, Practice Test 1 (Workbook Format)

_____ 1. E.
_____ 2. C. A teacher is in charge of a group of students, helping them learn and get better. A coach does the same thing, but does this with a group of players.
_____ 3. B. A frog is a tadpole before metamorphosis. A butterfly is a caterpillar before metamorphosis.
_____ 4. D. Opposites
_____ 5. E. A chef makes meals. A painter makes paintings.
_____ 6. E. A car is powered by gas. An oven is powered by electricity.
_____ 7. A. You should consume food if you are hungry. You should consume water if you are thirsty.
_____ 8. C. Both a brother and a son must be boys. In a family, a brother is the son of the parents. Both a sister and a daughter must be girls. In a family, a sister is the daughter of the parents.
_____ 9. D. You read a magazine. You listen to a radio. (The first word is the verb that goes with the second.)
_____ 10. C. These are "homophones": words that sound the same, but have different spellings and meanings.
_____ 11. C. A slide is found at a playground. A camel is found in a desert.
_____ 12. A. In a concert, a musician performs. In a movie, an actor performs.
_____ 13. E. Terrible can describe something very bad. Great can describe something very good.
_____ 14. D. A cow is a type of mammal. A toad is a type of amphibian.
_____ 15. B. Flowers are what make up a bouquet. Minutes are what make up hours.
_____ 16. B. The second word, beautiful, means very pretty. Tiny (the correct answer) means very small.
_____ 17. A. False is the opposite of true. Narrow is the opposite of wide.
_____ 18. E. Heat makes things warm. Rain makes things damp.
_____ 19. B. A lemon grows on a tree. A tomato grows on a vine.
_____ 20. D. You put eggs in a carton. You put flowers in a vase.
_____ 21. E. Liquid is the opposite of solid. Bright is the opposite of dim.
_____ 22. B. A tractor is used by people to ride around on a farm. A spaceship is used by people to ride around in outer space. A helicopter is not right because people cannot ride in outer space using them.

Verbal Analogies Questions Answered Correctly: _____ out of 22

Verbal Classification, p. 13, Practice Test 1 (Workbook Format)

_____ 1. D.   _____ 2. C. instruments   _____ 3. D. dairy products
_____ 4. B. people carry items in these things
_____ 5. A. help you see things close up; they have lenses to make things appear larger   _____ 6. D. seasons
_____ 7. C. animal homes   _____ 8. E. vehicles that travel in the air   _____ 9.B.continents
_____ 10. A. things that are yellow   _____ 11. B. parts of a plant
_____ 12. C. pretend characters that resemble people   _____ 13. E. insects   _____ 14. B. kitchen items
_____ 15. D. root vegetables   _____ 16. C. leg parts _____ 17. B. car parts _____ 18. C. types of birds
_____ 19. E. bodies of water   _____ 20. C. types of sports
_____ 21. D. flat/2D shapes (not 3D shapes)   _____ 22. A. countries

Verbal Classification Questions Answered Correctly: _____ out of 22

Sentence Completion, p. 16, Practice Test 1 (Workbook Format)

_____ 1. D. fierce = eager to fight   _____ 2. D. construct = build   _____ 3. B. discover = to find/make known
_____ 4. A. seldom = not often   _____ 5. C. demanding = needing a lot of effort, energy, and time
_____ 6. A. neutral = not supporting one side or another   _____ 7. B. toxic = poisonous
_____ 8. C. limited = not high in amount
_____ 9. B. yearned = to have really wanted something, often that you haven't been able to have/do
_____ 10. D. visualize = imagine   _____ 11. B. fascinating = very interesting
_____ 12. A. immense = very large   _____ 13. A. minuscule = very, very small
_____ 14. C. modern = present-day or recent   _____ 15. E. unethical = morally bad/ wrong
_____ 16. B. rival = competitor   _____ 17. D. temporary = not permanent
_____ 18. A. scarce = not enough for demand   _____ 19. E. covered = to have something over all the surface
_____ 20. C. significant = large enough to be noticed   _____ 21. E. collision = crash
_____ 22. B. landscape = the land/scenery of a particular area

Sentence Completion Questions Answered Correctly: _____ out of 22

Figure Analogies, p. 21, Practice Test 1 (Workbook Format)

_____ 1. C.   _____ 2. D. Top left & bottom right switch

_____ 3. E. On top, light blue star becomes an arrow filled with dots; bottom shape changes from dotted to light blue. In bottom set, the reverse: arrow filled with dots becomes a light blue star, bottom shape changes from light blue to dotted.

_____ 4. A. One arrow point is removed.

_____ 5. B. In top set, octagon design switches from gray to curved lines; the heart changes to a cross, changes position, and changes from curved lines to gray. In the bottom, the reverse occurs. The octagon changes from curved lines to gray. The heart changes to a cross & changes its position & design (gray to curved lines). No change w/ triangle.

_____ 6. B. Gray area becomes white & curved lines become gray area

_____ 7. D. From left to right, the pictures flip. (However, when you flip the bottom image, it appears the same.)

_____ 8. A. Arrow group rotates 90° clockwise,1 arrow is added.   _____ 9. C. Shape rotates 180°.

_____ 10. A. These switch: upper left, bottom right; Upper right, bottom left.

_____ 11. D. From left to right, 1/4 is removed.   _____ 12. E. Group of circles flips & 1 circle is added

_____ 13. A. Logic is "+1". In top set, a shape with +1 side appears. In bottom set there is +1 arrow.

_____ 14. B. One set of circles is removed & there are no black X's in the second set.

_____ 15. C. From left to right, there is the same shape. The white lines first make an "X" and then a cross. On bottom, it reverses, the white lines first make a cross and then an X.

_____ 16. B. Inside smaller shape moves from left to right & direction of lines switch.

_____ 17. D. Number of triangles decreases to 1 & this triangle has the same inside lines as the first 2 triangles.

_____ 18. E. A star is added on top of the shape/shape group.

_____ 19. B. Top shape goes inside bottom shape & gets bigger. Middle shape goes inside & rotates 90° clockwise.

Figure Analogies Questions Answered Correctly: _____ out of 19

Figure Classification, p. 28, Practice Test 1 (Workbook Format)

_____ 1. D.   _____ 2. D. Arrows with 1 point   _____ 3. E. Arrows pointing left

_____ 4. C. 4-sided shapes   _____ 5. B. Shapes alternate inside design

_____ 6. B. Larger circle with 1 octagon & 1 half-circle   _____ 7. A. 3 intersecting lines inside shape

_____ 8. C. 1 light blue hexagon in group of 3 shapes

_____ 9. D. 3 of the same shape align & face same direction horizontally; 1 small-1 large-1 small

_____ 10. D. 1 shape is oval, hexagon, or diamond; 1 shape with gray, dots, or diagonal lines

_____ 11. E. 8-sided shapes   _____ 12. B. Larger shape has 1 less side than the smaller inside shape

_____ 13. C. Combos of oval-diamond-trapezoid   _____ 14. A. 3 hearts in a row /tic-tac-toe

_____ 15. E. Shapes divided in half   _____ 16. B. Bottom shape rotates 90° counterclockwise

_____ 17. A. Square & triangle are across from another

_____ 18. E. Same smaller shape inside & part of larger shape has dots

Figure Classification Questions Answered Correctly: _____ out of 18

Paper Folding, p. 35, Practice Test 1 (Workbook Format)

_____ 1. D   _____ 2. E   _____ 3. D   _____ 4. C

_____ 5. C   _____ 6. B   _____ 7. C   _____ 8. A   _____ 9. C   _____ 10. E   _____ 11. B   _____ 12. A   _____ 13. D

_____ 14. C   _____ 15. B   _____ 16. B   _____ 17. E   Paper Folding Questions Answered Correctly: _____ out of 17

Number Puzzles, p. 41, Practice Test 1 (Workbook Format)

_____ 1. C   _____ 2. E   _____ 3. D   _____ 4. C

_____ 5. A   _____ 6. B   _____ 7. B   _____ 8. D   _____ 9. A   _____ 10. E   _____ 11. B   _____ 12. D   _____ 13. C

_____ 14. C   _____ 15. A   _____ 16. B   _____ 17. E   Number Puzzles Answered Correctly: _____ out of 17

Number Analogies, p. 45, Practice Test 1 (Workbook Format)

_____ 1. E. -1   _____ 2. B. ÷ by 2   _____ 3. D. +2

_____ 4. A. x3   _____ 5. B. +5   _____ 6. B. ÷ by 4   _____ 7. C. x10   _____ 8. A. +7   _____ 9. C. x2

_____ 10. D. -9   _____ 11. E. -7   _____ 12. D.+4   _____ 13. E. -3   _____ 14. A. x5   _____ 15. D. +9

_____ 16. C. ÷ by 3   _____ 17. C. -5   _____ 18. B. ÷ by 2   Number Analogies Answered Correctly: _____ out of 18

Number Series, p. 50, Practice Test 1 (Workbook Format)

_____ 1.D.   _____ 2. E.

_____ 3. D. rods 1,3,5,7 incr. by 1; rods 2,4,6 have 7   _____ 4. D. rods 1,3,5,7 incr. by 2; rods 2,4,6 incr. by 2

_____ 5. A. 4-3-6-0-4-3-6   _____ 6. C. rods 1,3,5,7 & rods 2, 4, 6 incr. by 2   _____ 7. A. 1-0-0-1-0-0

_____ 8. B. rods 1,3,5,7 decr. by 2; rods 2,4,6 decr. by 2.   _____ 9. A. -5   _____ 10. B. +1,+2,+1,+2,etc.

_____ 11. D. -1, -2, -1, -2, etc.   _____ 12. D. +2, +4, +2, +4, etc.   _____ 13. C. +3, -4, +3, -4, etc.

_____ 14. A. +3, +0 (or, same), +3, +0 (or, same)   _____ 15. E. +1.0 (or, +1)   _____ 16. D. +0.05

_____ 17. E. -1,-1,-2,-1,-1,-2   _____ 18. B. +9   _____ 19. C. +1.5

Number Series Answered Correctly: _____ out of 19

Verbal Analogies, p. 56, Practice Test 2

_____ 1. C. A mechanic would fix an engine. A plumber would fix a drain.   _____ 2. E. Opposites
_____ 3. A. A river is similar to a creek, but a river is larger than a creek. A cavern and cave are similar, but a cavern is larger than a cave.
_____ 4. D. People have hair, which on animals (like dogs and cats), compares to fur. People have feet, which on animals (like dogs and cats), compares to paws.
_____ 5. B. Animal > Sound animal makes   _____ 6. C. Continent > Ocean bordering that continent
_____ 7. B. Word > same word spelled backwards
_____ 8. A. A ruler is used to measure length. A compass is used to measure direction (by showing which way is north).
_____ 9. D. A house's top part is the attic. A mountain's top part is the peak.
_____ 10. A. A peacock & owl are birds; shark & tuna are fish.
_____ 11. C. A unit of measurement for weight is a pound. A unit of measurement for temperature is a degree.
_____ 12. B. Innocent is the opposite of guilty. Success is the opposite of failure.
_____ 13. E. A hand is used to feel. A mouth is used to taste.
_____ 14. E. All are countries.   _____ 15. C. Lettuce is a vegetable. An acorn is a nut.
_____ 16. B. A monkey and a horse are mammals. A turtle and a lizard are reptiles.
_____ 17. E. A carriage provides a slower form of transport than a car. A car has a motor. Both usually have 4 wheels. A bicycle provides a slower form of transport than a motorcycle. A motorcycle has a motor. Both usually have 2 wheels.
_____ 18. D. A chainsaw is a motorized version of saw. A chainsaw does the same thing as a saw, but faster. The same is true of a drill and screwdriver.
_____ 19. A. Bread is made from grain. Paper is made from a tree.
_____ 20. B. Twins are two brothers/sisters born at the same time. A pair is made up of 2 similar things. Triplets are three brothers/sisters born at the same time. A trio is made up of 3 similar things.
Verbal Analogies Questions Answered Correctly: _____ out of 20

Verbal Classification, p. 58, Practice Test 2

_____ 1. D. colors   _____ 2. E. places people live   _____ 3. A. languages
_____ 4. C. actions of the 5 senses   _____ 5. E. things used to measure   _____ 6. B. things worn on head
_____ 7. C. things that you step on to that take you up or down to another level
_____ 8. E. all begin with letter "S"
_____ 9. D. utensils used to put food in mouth (the others are not utensils to put food in mouth)
_____ 10. C. major oceans of the world (Arctic, Atlantic, Indian, Pacific, and Southern)
_____ 11. A. kinds of roads   _____ 12. C. emotions you feel when you are happy
_____ 13. D. things that come in pairs (2's)
_____ 14. B. mammals (It is important to notice that the answer is not any of the choices that start with "R" because there is more than one choice that starts with "R".)
_____ 15. A. types of plants (algae is not technically a kind of plant, also, algae grows in water, or where it is very wet; the items in the question grow on land)
_____ 16. E. feelings associated with wanting to sleep
_____ 17. C. things that measure time _____ 18. C. things used to cut
_____ 19. A. liquids   _____ 20. D. animals that have shells
Verbal Classification Questions Answered Correctly: _____ out of 20

Sentence Completion, p. 60, Practice Test 2

_____ 1. B. focused = to pay much attention to   _____ 2. D. vary = to change
_____ 3. E. geometry = the study of shapes, sizes, dimensions   _____ 4. A. loss = to no longer have something
_____ 5. C. nutrients = healthy substances that help you live/grow   _____ 6. A. repay = to pay back
_____ 7. B. hectic = with lots of activity/non-stop   _____ 8. D. border = a line separating countries
_____ 9. E. furious = very mad
_____ 10. A. private = only for 1 group, not public   _____ 11. E. astonishing = very surprising
_____ 12. B. ration = to allow people to only have a certain amount of something
_____ 13. C. complete = finish
_____ 14. D. abstract = here, art that does not show something how it really looks, but represents it using various colors, shapes, figures
_____ 15. B. descendant = someone who is descended from (related to) an ancestor (a relative, usually older than one's grandparent)
_____ 16. D. permanent = lasting/not changing   _____ 17. B. vacant = empty
_____ 18. E. connected = joined   _____ 19. C. approval = permission
_____ 20. A. burden = something that is not enjoyable or that is difficult that you must deal with
Sentence Completion Questions Answered Correctly: _____ out of 20

Figure Analogies, p. 64, Practice Test 2

____ 1. E. Shapes align largest to smallest & turn blue   ____ 2. C. White to gray/gray to white
____ 3. A. # of arrow points = # of shape sides
____ 4. B. Dotted to gray; black to dotted; gray to black -OR- bottom shape moves to top & the other 2 move down
____ 5. A. From left to right, larger shape +1 side, smaller shape +1 side; colors of large & small shape reverse
____ 6. B. Small shape turns dark & rotates 90°_   ____ 7. E. Small shape from group becomes large
____ 8. D. From left to right: same group of shapes w/ small vertically-aligned gray circles in middle
____ 9. D. Designs/colors of small & large shapes switch ____ 10. C. From left to right: an oval is added to shape group.
____ 11. B. Larger shape the color of smaller shape
____ 12. A. Inner shape gets larger, wider; outer shape gets smaller, turns light blue, touches large shape's borders
____ 13. D. Outer dotted shape gets small inside 1st box's inner shape   14. ____ C. # of shapes decreases by 1
____ 15. A. The right side of the question box has 1 shape from the group of 2 shapes on the left side of the question box. It's the shape on the group's right side & it turns to light blue.
____ 16. C. Larger shape gains 1 side; Design of larger/smaller shape switch
____ 17. A. White shape increases & light blue shape decreases with smaller version on top of larger version
____ 18. C. Black to white/ white to black   Figure Analogies Questions Answered Correctly: _____ out of 18

Figure Classification, p. 70, Practice Test 2

____ 1. A. Figures of same size   ____ 2. C. Rounded shapes
____ 3. C. Circle and rectangle next to each other   ____ 4. A. Dotted lines from upper left to lower right
____ 5. E. Single straight line at same point on figure ____ 6. C. 1/4 filled with dots
____ 7. E. 1 shape each: curvy lines, dark color, or dotted lines ____ 8. B. Octagon is next to parallelogram; star isn't
____ 9. D. Circle divided into equal parts   ____ 10. A. 3 down triangles, 1 up triangle
____ 11. D. Flat base, round-top shape in middle   ____ 12. A. Pyramid, cube, cuboid w/ white, black, gray
____ 13. A. Same arrow-half has dots as it rotates 90° counterclockwise ____ 14. B. Divided in 1/2 upper left to lower right
____ 15. E. U,A,W in black, gray, & vertical lines   ____ 16. C. Triangles w/ different color square inside
____ 17. D. 2 same-color shapes in rounded shape   ____ 18. C. 3 shapes
                          Figure Classification Questions Answered Correctly: _____ out of 18

Paper Folding, p. 76, Practice Test 2

____ 1. B   ____ 2. C   ____ 3. D   ____ 4. E   ____ 5. D   ____ 6. E   ____ 7. C   ____ 8. A   ____ 9. B
____ 10. B   ____ 11. C   ____ 12. E   ____ 13. C   ____ 14. E   ____ 15. A
                                  Paper Folding Answered Correctly: _____ out of 15

Number Puzzles, p. 81, Practice Test 2

____ 1. A   ____ 2. E   ____ 3. B   ____ 4. D   ____ 5. B   ____ 6. C   ____ 7. C   ____ 8. B   ____ 9. E
____ 10. B   ____ 11. C   ____ 12. D   ____ 13. A   ____ 14. E   ____ 15. B   ____ 16. D   ____ 17. C   ____ 18. E
____ 19. B   ____ 20. B
                          Number Puzzles Questions Answered Correctly: _____ out of 20

Number Analogies, p. 85, Practice Test 2

____ 1. B. -8   ____ 2. A. +6   ____ 3. E. +10   ____ 4. C. x2   ____ 5. D. x4   ____ 6. B. ÷ by 3   ____ 7. D. +8
____ 8. C. -2   ____ 9. B. -6   ____ 10. A. +3   ____ 11. C. -4   ____ 12. E. -10   ____ 13. B. +7   ____ 14. E. +2
____ 15. C. ÷ by 10   ____ 16. B. mult by 3   ____ 17. D. ÷ by 4   ____ 18. A. ÷ by 5
                          Number Analogies Questions Answered Correctly: _____ out of 18

Number Series - Abacus, p. 89, Practice Test 2

____ 1. D. Rows 2,4,6 incr. by 2; rows 1,3,5 = "0"   ____ 2. A. Rows 1,3,5 and rows 2,4,6 decr. by 1
____ 3. B. 7-6-5-0-5-6   ____ 4. C. Rows 1,3,5,7 decr. by 1; rows 2,4,6 = "0"
____ 5. D. Rows 1,3,5,7 decr. by 1; rows 2,4,6 incr. by 1   ____ 6. D. 2-5-6-2-5-6

Number Series - Text, p. 91, Practice Test 2

____ 1. E. +3   ____ 2. A. +12   ____ 3. B. +2,+1,+2,+1, etc.
____ 4. C. in places 1,3,5,7 there's a "1"; in places 2,4,6 you add +2   ____ 5. E. -11
____ 6. A. +0 (or, same), +2, +0 (or, same), +2, +0 (or, same), +2   ____ 7. B. -0.5
____ 8. D. +1, +8, +1, +8, +1, +8   ____ 9. E. +1, +1, +2, +1, +1, +2   ____ 10. C. -1.0 (or, -1)
____ 11. B. +10, +2, +10, +2, etc.   ____ 12. A. -2, +3, -2, +3, etc.
                          Number Series Questions Answered Correctly: _____ out of 18
                          (6 Abacus, 12 Text)

Ready for test day?

Check out more COGAT® books at

www.GatewayGifted.com

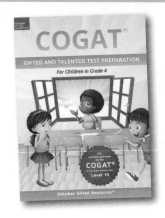

Visit www.GatewayGifted.com/math

for a free COGAT® grade 3 math eBook.

Great Work!

Congratulations To:

Points Earned:

_____